This Book Belongs to:

REUDOR's

THE DOODLED FAMILY™ HAGGADAH

ATARA PUBLISHING

This book was made possible by the joint efforts of
Jeff "Magik Mouse" Coen
Jeff "Magik Mouse" Coen
(He gets mentioned twice because he worked twice as hard as anyone)
"Jumpin' Josh Flash" Coen
Burt "Offerings" Griswald
Jack "The Black" Knight
Steven "Rocket Boy" Wollman
Roderick "G-Force Man" Peace
Dafna and Elisha "Are we there yet" Gilboa
The Doodles (Effie & Cari & Ariel & Shira & Gilad)
Moshe Rabbeinu

ISBN 1-886611-22-X
North American Distribution by Alef Judaica, Inc.
Culver City, California
Published by Atara Publishing
Huntington Beach, California.

In Loving Memory of My Mother

Atara Gratch עטרה גרטש

זכרונה לברכה

1.

2.

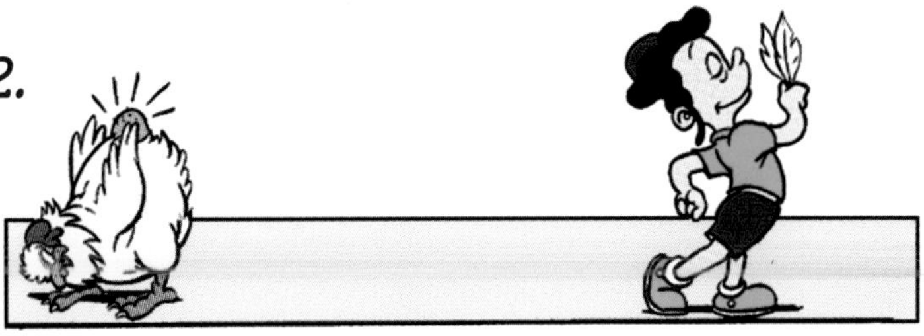

CHAMETZ is a mixture of flour and water which rises and becomes bread. To make matzah even more special during Pesach, we don't eat or own any Chametz during the holiday. For this reason, we clean and scrub the house during the weeks before Pesach to make sure we get rid of all Chametz. On the evening before the holiday (except if it begins on Saturday night, in which case, the following would be done on Thursday night), we inspect the house one last time. To make the search more exciting, we place 10 pieces of Chametz throughout the house. We then turn off the lights, light a candle and say:

בָּרוּךְ אַתָּה יְיָ, אֱלֹהֵינוּ מֶלֶךְ הָעוֹלָם, אֲשֶׁר קִדְּשָׁנוּ בְּמִצְוֹתָיו, וְצִוָּנוּ עַל בִּעוּר חָמֵץ.

Blessed are you, King of the universe, Who has sanctified us by His commandments and commanded us concerning the removal of chametz.

The search is on! To the light of the burning candle, search out each piece of Chametz and whisk it with a feather onto a wooden spoon and then into a paper bag. Make sure you get every last crumb! Now say:

כָּל חֲמִירָא וַחֲמִיעָא, דְּאִכָּא בִרְשׁוּתִי, דַּחֲזִיתֵּה וּדְלָא חֲזִיתֵּה, דַּחֲמִיתֵּה, וּדְלָא
חֲמִיתֵּה, דְּבַעֲרְתֵּה וּדְלָא בַעֲרְתֵּה, לִבְּטֵל וְלֶהֱוֵי הֶפְקֵר כְּעַפְרָא דְאַרְעָא.

Any chametz which is in my possession which I didn't see, remove, or know about, should be void and become ownerless, like the dust of the earth.

The next morning, burn all the remaining chametz and say:

כָּל חֲמִירָא
וַחֲמִיעָא דְּאִכָּא
בִרְשׁוּתִי דַּחֲזִיתֵּה
וּדְלָא חֲזִיתֵּה
דַּחֲמִיתֵּה וּדְלָא
חֲמִיתֵּה דְּבַעֲרְתֵּה
וּדְלָא בַעֲרְתֵּה
לִבְּטֵל וְלֶהֱוֵי
הֶפְקֵר כְּעַפְרָא
דְאַרְעָא.

That's not quite what I meant by getting rid of the Chametz!

Any chametz which is in my possession which I didn't see or remove, should be void and become ownerless, like the dust of the earth.

CHAMETZ also symbolizes the *yetzer ha-ra* — the evil inclination. Going through the trouble of removing all Chametz from our home reminds us of how difficult it is to overcome and get rid of our own bad habits. Just like the Israelites were freed from slavery in Egypt, we are freed from being enslaved by negative things.
We also compare Chametz to pride, because leavened bread is puffed up. Pharaoh thought of himself as a god and had to be humbled by the 10 plagues. So every year, we search for and remove the little pieces of Pharaoh's arrogance which may lie within us.

ERUV TAVSHILIN

When Passover falls on Friday, the following is said in order to permit food preparation on the holiday for the Sabbath Set aside matzah and cooked food, and say:

Blessed are You, God, King of the universe, Who sanctified us by His commandments and commanded us concerning the commandments of the Eruv.

Through this Eruv, may we be able to bake, cook, fry, insulate, kindle flame, prepare for, and do anything necessary for Shabbat on the holiday — for ourselves and for all the Jews living in this city.

ערוב תבשילין.

בָּרוּךְ אַתָּה יְיָ, אֱלֹהֵינוּ מֶלֶךְ הָעוֹלָם, אֲשֶׁר קִדְּשָׁנוּ בְּמִצְוֹתָיו וְצִוָּנוּ עַל מִצְוַת עֵרוּב

בְּהָדֵין עֵרוּבָא יְהֵא שָׁרֵא לָנָא לְמֵיפֵא, וּלְבַשָּׁלָא, וּלְאַצְלָיָא וּלְאַטְמָנָא וּלְאַדְלָקָא שְׁרָגָא וּלְמֶעְבַּד כָּל צָרְכָּנָא, מִיּוֹמָא טָבָא לְשַׁבְּתָא. לָנוּ, וּלְכָל יִשְׂרָאֵל, הַדָּרִים בָּעִיר הַזֹּאת.

3.

4.

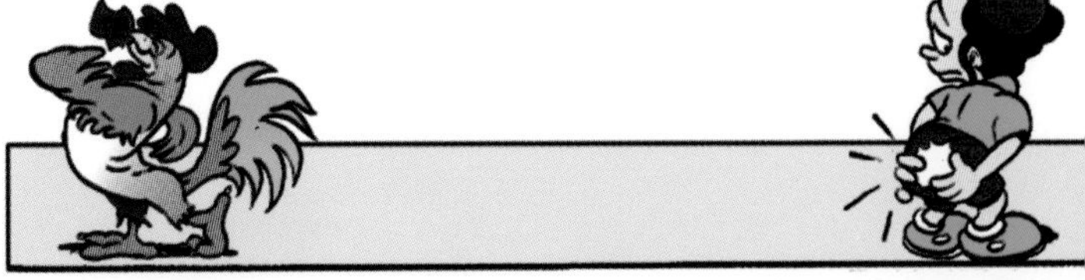

The seder table is set with the finest utensils, as a reminder that Israel left Egypt with plenty of riches.

THE SEDER TABLE

Before beginning the ceremony, make sure you have the following items on the seder table:

HAGGADOT — Everyone should have his own Haggadah.

CANDLE STICKS — Use long candles so that they last as long as possible during the seder night.

MATZOT — Place three specially baked Passover matzot on a plate atop each other, and then cover them.

WINE — Make sure you use Kosher for Passover wine or grape juice and have enough on hand for everyone to fill four cups. Each cup reminds us of the four ways God said he would free the Israelites, as it says in Exodus 6:6-7, "I will take you out," "I will save you," "I will redeem you," and "I will take you to be my people."

ELIJAH'S CUP — Some rabbis say that we should drink *five* cups of wine during the seder because in addition to the above redemptions, it says in Exodus 6:8, "I will bring you." Since Elijah the Prophet is expected to arrive on a seder night and announce the arrival of the Messiah, we fill a fifth cup but don't drink it, hoping Elijah settles the dispute when he arrives.

SALT WATER — A symbol of the tears of slavery, we use the salt water for dipping our Karpas. You may want to use more than one dish so that everyone can reach it.

Place the seder plate as shown at the head of the table so that the leader can easily reach it throughout the seder.

THE SEDER PLATE

קערה של פסח

BETZAH

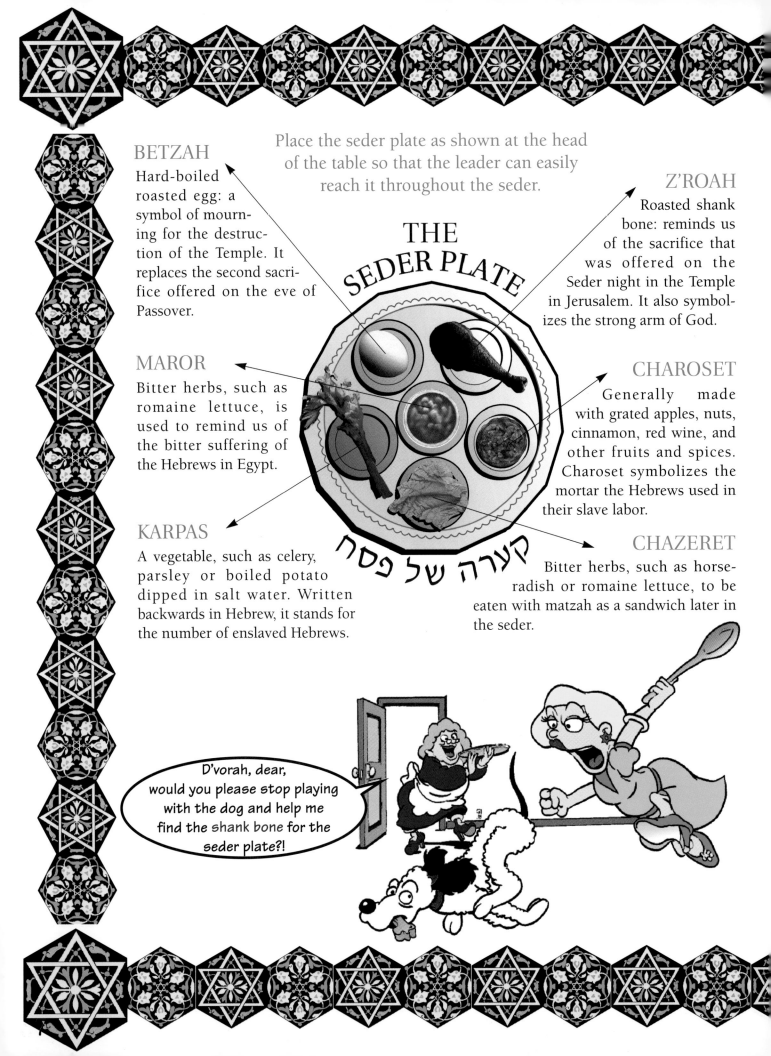

Hard-boiled roasted egg: a symbol of mourning for the destruction of the Temple. It replaces the second sacrifice offered on the eve of Passover.

MAROR

Bitter herbs, such as romaine lettuce, is used to remind us of the bitter suffering of the Hebrews in Egypt.

KARPAS

A vegetable, such as celery, parsley or boiled potato dipped in salt water. Written backwards in Hebrew, it stands for the number of enslaved Hebrews.

Z'ROAH

Roasted shank bone: reminds us of the sacrifice that was offered on the Seder night in the Temple in Jerusalem. It also symbolizes the strong arm of God.

CHAROSET

Generally made with grated apples, nuts, cinnamon, red wine, and other fruits and spices. Charoset symbolizes the mortar the Hebrews used in their slave labor.

CHAZERET

Bitter herbs, such as horseradish or romaine lettuce, to be eaten with matzah as a sandwich later in the seder.

D'vorah, dear, would you please stop playing with the dog and help me find the shank bone for the seder plate?!

ORDER OF THE SEDER סימני הסדר

On Friday night begin: And there was evening and there was morning,the sixth day. So the heaven and the earth were finished, and everything in them. On the seventh day God finished His work which He had done, and He rested on the seventh day. God blessed the seventh day and made it holy, because on it He rested from all His work. *On all other nights:* With your permission, my masters and teachers Blessed are You, God, King of the universe, Who creates the fruit of the vine.Blessed are You, God, King of the universe, Who has chosen us from all nations, honored us above all peoples, and blessed us with His commandments. And You, God, have lovingly given us (Sabbaths for rest), special times for gladness, feasts and seasons for joy, (this Sabbath and) this Feast of Matzos, the season of our freedom (in love), a holy celebration in memory of the Exodus from Egypt. Because You have chosen and blessed us above all peoples, (and the Sabbath) and You have given us as a tradition Your holy festivals (in love and favor), in gladness and joy. Blessed are You, GOD, Who makes (the Sabbath) holy, Israel, and the holiday seasons. *On Saturday night:* Blessed are You, God, King of the universe, Who creates the light of the fire. Blessed are You, God, King of the universe, Who makes a separation between the holy and non-holy, between light and darkness, between Israel and other peoples, between the seventh day and the six days of the week. You have made a separation between the holiness of the Sabbath and the holiness of a Holiday, and have made the seventh day more holy than the six days of the week. You separated and blessed Your nation, Israel, with Your holiness. Blessed are You, God, Who separates between holiness and holiness.

וַיְהִי עֶרֶב וַיְהִי בֹקֶר יוֹם הַשִּׁשִּׁי, וַיְכֻלּוּ הַשָּׁמַיִם וְהָאָרֶץ וְכָל צְבָאָם: וַיְכַל אֱלֹהִים בַּיּוֹם הַשְּׁבִיעִי, מְלַאכְתּוֹ אֲשֶׁר עָשָׂה, וַיִּשְׁבֹּת בַּיּוֹם הַשְּׁבִיעִי, מִכָּל מְלַאכְתּוֹ אֲשֶׁר עָשָׂה. וַיְבָרֶךְ אֱלֹהִים אֶת יוֹם הַשְּׁבִיעִי, וַיְקַדֵּשׁ אֹתוֹ, כִּי בוֹ שָׁבַת מִכָּל מְלַאכְתּוֹ, אֲשֶׁר בָּרָא אֱלֹהִים לַעֲשׂוֹת.

סָבְרֵי מָרָנָן וְרַבָּנָן וְרַבּוֹתַי:

בָּרוּךְ אַתָּה יְיָ, אֱלֹהֵינוּ מֶלֶךְ הָעוֹלָם, בּוֹרֵא פְּרִי הַגָּפֶן.

בָּרוּךְ אַתָּה יְיָ, אֱלֹהֵינוּ מֶלֶךְ הָעוֹלָם, אֲשֶׁר בָּחַר בָּנוּ מִכָּל עָם, וְרוֹמְמָנוּ מִכָּל לָשׁוֹן, וְקִדְּשָׁנוּ בְּמִצְוֹתָיו, וַתִּתֶּן לָנוּ יְיָ אֱלֹהֵינוּ בְּאַהֲבָה (לשבת שַׁבָּתוֹת לִמְנוּחָה וּ) מוֹעֲדִים לְשִׂמְחָה, חַגִּים וּזְמַנִּים לְשָׂשׂוֹן אֶת יוֹם (הַשַּׁבָּת הַזֶּה, וְאֶת יוֹם) חַג הַמַּצּוֹת הַזֶּה. זְמַן חֵרוּתֵנוּ, (בְּאַהֲבָה) מִקְרָא קֹדֶשׁ. זֵכֶר לִיצִיאַת מִצְרָיִם. כִּי בָנוּ בָחַרְתָּ וְאוֹתָנוּ קִדַּשְׁתָּ מִכָּל הָעַמִּים. (וְשַׁבָּת) וּמוֹעֲדֵי קָדְשְׁךָ (בְּאַהֲבָה וּבְרָצוֹן) בְּשִׂמְחָה וּבְשָׂשׂוֹן הִנְחַלְתָּנוּ. בָּרוּךְ אַתָּה יְיָ, מְקַדֵּשׁ (הַשַּׁבָּת וְ) יִשְׂרָאֵל וְהַזְּמַנִּים.

On Saturday add:

בָּרוּךְ אַתָּה יְיָ, אֱלֹהֵינוּ מֶלֶךְ הָעוֹלָם, בּוֹרֵא מְאוֹרֵי הָאֵשׁ.

בָּרוּךְ אַתָּה יְיָ, לאֱלֹהֵינוּ מֶלֶךְ הָעוֹלָם, הַמַּבְדִּיל בֵּין קֹדֶשׁ לְחֹל בֵּין אוֹר לְחֹשֶׁךְ, בֵּין יִשְׂרָאֵל לָעַמִּים, בֵּין יוֹם הַשְּׁבִיעִי לְשֵׁשֶׁת יְמֵי הַמַּעֲשֶׂה. בֵּין קְדֻשַּׁת שַׁבָּת לִקְדֻשַּׁת יוֹם טוֹב הִבְדַּלְתָּ. וְאֶת יוֹם הַשְּׁבִיעִי מִשֵּׁשֶׁת יְמֵי הַמַּעֲשֶׂה קִדַּשְׁתָּ. הִבְדַּלְתָּ וְקִדַּשְׁתָּ אֶת עַמְּךָ יִשְׂרָאֵל בִּקְדֻשָּׁתֶךָ. בָּרוּךְ אַתָּה יְיָ, הַמַּבְדִּיל בֵּין קֹדֶשׁ לְקֹדֶשׁ.

Drink while reclining to the left.

MOMMMMMMMM!
Tell Oody to stop reclining all over me!

בָּרוּךְ אַתָּה יְיָ, אֱלֹהֵינוּ מֶלֶךְ הָעוֹלָם, שֶׁהֶחֱיָנוּ וְקִיְּמָנוּ וְהִגִּיעָנוּ לַזְּמַן הַזֶּה.

Blessed are You, God, King of the universe, Who has kept us alive, nourished us, and brought us to this season.

וּרְחַץ

WASH THE HANDS

We wash our hands, but don't say the blessing, since we won't be eating for a while.
OH, NO!, please don't let me starve!

כַּרְפַּס

DIP AND EAT A VEGETABLE

Dip a vegetable into salt water.

בָּרוּךְ אַתָּה יְיָ, אֱלֹהֵינוּ מֶלֶךְ הָעוֹלָם, בּוֹרֵא פְּרִי הָאֲדָמָה.

Blessed are You, God, King of the universe, Who creates the fruit of the earth.

יַחַץ

BREAK THE MIDDLE MATZAH

The head of the home breaks the middle matzah in two. The smaller part is put back and the larger part is used as the Afikoman.

Trudy, you search the cabinets! Bitsy: under the furniture! If all else fails, we'll ambush Dad and squeeze the location of the Afikoman out of him!

מַגִּיד

PASSOVER STORY

The reason we lift the Matzahs must be so the kids won't get to it!

Lift the matzahs for all to see, and say aloud:

הָא לַחְמָא עַנְיָא דִּי אֲכַלוּ אַבְהָתַנָא בְּאַרְעָא
דְמִצְרָיִם. כָּל דִּכְפִין יֵיתֵי וְיֵכֻל, כָּל דִּצְרִיךְ יֵיתֵי
וְיִפְסַח. הַשַּׁתָּא הָכָא, לְשָׁנָה הַבָּאָה בְּאַרְעָה
דְיִשְׂרָאֵל. הַשַּׁתָּא עַבְדֵי, לְשָׁנָה הַבָּאָה בְּנֵי חוֹרִין.

This is the bread of hardship that our ancestors ate in the land of Egypt. Whoever is hungry — let him come and eat! Whoever is needy — let him come and celebrate Passover! Now, we are here; next year we hope to be in the Land of Israel! Now, we are slaves; next year we hope to be free men!

"Pick a Matzah...any Matzah!"

- Sometimes, the three matzot are referred to as Kohen, Levi and Israel, after the three types of Jews.
- Others say the matzot represent our three patriarchs: Abraham, Isaac and Jacob.
- The Jews of Kochin, India, mark the different matzot with lines: the Kohen with two, the Levi with three and the Israel with four. They skip one line because only God is one.
- The word Afikoman originated from a Greek word meaning dessert.

At the end of the meal, just before the Afikoman, the Jews of Morocco put on their shoes, a belt, take a staff in their hands, place the wrapped Afikoman over their shoulders and walk a few paces with it, literally following the words in the Torah.

מה נשתנה הלילה הזה

Take away the Seder plate and pour the second of the four cups of wine.
The youngest at the table asks the reasons why we are doing things differently tonight.

Why is this night different from all other nights?

מַה נִּשְׁתַּנָּה הַלַּיְלָה הַזֶּה מִכָּל הַלֵּילוֹת?

1. ON ALL OTHER NIGHTS we eat chametz and matzah, but on this night — only matzah.

1. שֶׁבְּכָל הַלֵּילוֹת אָנוּ אוֹכְלִין חָמֵץ וּמַצָּה, הַלַּיְלָה הַזֶּה - כֻּלּוֹ מַצָּה.

2. ON ALL OTHER NIGHTS we eat many vegetables, but on this night — we eat maror.

2. שֶׁבְּכָל הַלֵּילוֹת אָנוּ אוֹכְלִין שְׁאָר יְרָקוֹת, הַלַּיְלָה הַזֶּה - מָרוֹר.

3. ON ALL OTHER NIGHTS we do not dip even once, but on this night — twice.

3. שֶׁבְּכָל הַלֵּילוֹת אֵין אָנוּ מַטְבִּילִין אֲפִילוּ פַּעַם אֶחָת, הַלַּיְלָה הַזֶּה - שְׁתֵּי פְעָמִים.

4. ON ALL OTHER NIGHTS we eat either sitting or reclining, but on this night — we all recline.

4. שֶׁבְּכָל הַלֵּילוֹת אָנוּ אוֹכְלִין בֵּין יוֹשְׁבִין וּבֵין מְסֻבִּין, הַלַּיְלָה הַזֶּה - כֻּלָּנוּ מְסֻבִּין.

Put the Seder plate back on the table.
Keep the matzahs uncovered while everyone reads together:

Mommy nanna Alalala zay Nicole la-le-lo! ...I have to go potty!
Why is this night different than all other nights? A rhetorical question? I think not! Philosophically speaking, these four questions represent the essence of a nation's intrinsic drive to prevail over adversity and pursue a more harmonious physical existence on a loftier spiritual plane! The spirit of freedom triumphs over the maror! Waves of brotherhood wash away the salt water! And compassion topples even the grandest structures built with the villainous mortar!
Monies – ton of! I'll lie low as hay Me haul all the loot!

עֲבָדִים הָיִינוּ לְפַרְעֹה בְּמִצְרָיִם. וַיּוֹצִיאֵנוּ
יְיָ אֱלֹהֵינוּ מִשָּׁם, בְּיָד חֲזָקָה וּבִזְרוֹעַ נְטוּיָה,
וְאִלּוּ לֹא הוֹצִיא הַקָּדוֹשׁ בָּרוּךְ הוּא אֶת
אֲבוֹתֵינוּ מִמִּצְרַיִם, הֲרֵי אָנוּ וּבָנֵינוּ וּבְנֵי בָנֵינוּ,
מְשֻׁעְבָּדִים הָיִינוּ לְפַרְעֹה בְּמִצְרָיִם. וַאֲפִילוּ
כֻּלָּנוּ חֲכָמִים, כֻּלָּנוּ נְבוֹנִים, כֻּלָּנוּ זְקֵנִים,
כֻּלָּנוּ יוֹדְעִים אֶת הַתּוֹרָה, מִצְוָה עָלֵינוּ לְסַפֵּר
בִּיצִיאַת מִצְרָיִם. וְכָל הַמַּרְבֶּה לְסַפֵּר בִּיצִיאַת
מִצְרַיִם, הֲרֵי זֶה מְשֻׁבָּח.

מַעֲשֶׂה בְּרַבִּי אֱלִיעֶזֶר, וְרַבִּי יְהוֹשֻׁעַ, וְרַבִּי
אֶלְעָזָר בֶּן עֲזַרְיָה, וְרַבִּי עֲקִיבָא, וְרַבִּי טַרְפוֹן,
שֶׁהָיוּ מְסֻבִּין בִּבְנֵי-בְרַק, וְהָיוּ מְסַפְּרִים
בִּיצִיאַת מִצְרַיִם, כָּל אוֹתוֹ הַלַּיְלָה, עַד שֶׁבָּאוּ
תַלְמִידֵיהֶם וְאָמְרוּ לָהֶם: רַבּוֹתֵינוּ, הִגִּיעַ
זְמַן קְרִיאַת שְׁמַע, שֶׁל שַׁחֲרִית.

We were slaves to Pharaoh in Egypt, but God rescued us with a mighty hand and an outstretched arm. If he didn't rescue our ancestors from Egypt, then we, our children, and our children's children would have stayed there as slaves to Pharaoh in Egypt. Even if we were all wise, understanding, experienced, and knowledgeable of the Torah, we would still need to tell about the Exodus from Egypt. The more one tells about the Exodus, the more he is praised.

Once, Rabbi Eliezer, Rabbi Yehoshua, Rabbi Elazar ben Azaryah, Rabbi Akiva, and Rabbi Tarfon were at the Seder in Bnei Brak. They talked about the Exodus all that night until their students came and said to them: 'Our teachers, it is daybreak and time to read the morning Shema.'

אָמַר רַבִּי אֶלְעָזָר בֶּן-עֲזַרְיָה. הֲרֵי אֲנִי כְּבֶן שִׁבְעִים שָׁנָה, וְלֹא זָכִיתִי, שֶׁתֵּאָמֵר יְצִיאַת מִצְרַיִם בַּלֵּילוֹת. עַד שֶׁדְּרָשָׁהּ בֶּן זוֹמָא. שֶׁנֶּאֱמַר: לְמַעַן תִּזְכֹּר, אֶת יוֹם צֵאתְךָ מֵאֶרֶץ מִצְרַיִם, כֹּל יְמֵי חַיֶּיךָ. יְמֵי חַיֶּיךָ הַיָּמִים. כֹּל יְמֵי חַיֶּיךָ הַלֵּילוֹת. וַחֲכָמִים אוֹמְרִים: יְמֵי חַיֶּיךָ הָעוֹלָם הַזֶּה. כֹּל יְמֵי חַיֶּיךָ לְהָבִיא לִימוֹת הַמָּשִׁיחַ.

Rabbi Elazar ben Azaryah said: I am like a seventy-year-old man, but I could not succeed in having the Exodus from Egypt mentioned every night, until Ben Zoma explained it: 'So that you may remember the day you left Egypt all the days of your life'. The phrase 'the days of your life' would have meant only the days; the addition of the word 'all,' includes the nights as well. But the Sages say that 'the days of your life' would mean only the present world; the addition of 'all' includes the time of the Messiah.

RABBI EIZEL CHARIF WOULD SAY, "WHAT WAS THE DIFFERENCE BETWEEN THE GENERATION OF THOSE WHO LEFT EGYPT AND OUR GENERATION? THEY DISPOSED OF THEIR GOLD AND SILVER TO MAKE A GOD, WHILE IN OUR GENERATION PEOPLE DISPOSE OF GOD IN ORDER TO MAKE GOLD AND SILVER.

Blessed is the powerful one; blessed is He. Blessed is the One Who gave the Torah to His people Israel; blessed is He. The Torah speaks of four sons: a WISE one, a WICKED one, a SIMPLE one, and one WHO IS UNABLE TO ASK.

בָּרוּךְ הַמָּקוֹם. בָּרוּךְ הוּא. בָּרוּךְ שֶׁנָּתַן תּוֹרָה לְעַמּוֹ יִשְׂרָאֵל. בָּרוּךְ הוּא. כְּנֶגֶד אַרְבָּעָה בָנִים דִּבְּרָה תוֹרָה. אֶחָד חָכָם, וְאֶחָד רָשָׁע, וְאֶחָד תָּם, וְאֶחָד שֶׁאֵינוֹ יוֹדֵעַ לִשְׁאוֹל.

חָכָם

THE WISE SON — what does he say? 'What are the statements, orders, and rulings which God commanded you?.' So explain to him the laws of the Passover offering: that one may not eat dessert after the final taste of the Passover offering.

מַה הוּא אוֹמֵר? מָה הָעֵדֹת וְהַחֻקִּים וְהַמִּשְׁפָּטִים, אֲשֶׁר צִוָּה יְיָ אֱלֹהֵינוּ אֶתְכֶם? וְאַף אַתָּה אֱמָר לוֹ כְּהִלְכוֹת הַפֶּסַח: אֵין מַפְטִירִין אַחַר הַפֶּסַח אֲפִיקוֹמָן.

רָשָׁע

THE WICKED SON — what does he say? 'What purpose is this work to you?' He says, 'To you', not including himself. By setting himself apart from those who believe in the Torah, he goes against the basic belief of Judaism. We should scold him and say: 'For this reason, God did so for me when I went out of Egypt.' 'For me,' but not for him — had he been there, he would not have been rescued.

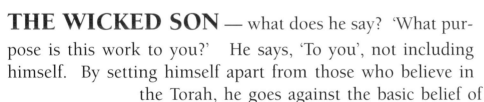

מַה הוּא אוֹמֵר? מָה הָעֲבֹדָה הַזֹּאת לָכֶם? לָכֶם וְלֹא לוֹ. וּלְפִי שֶׁהוֹצִיא אֶת עַצְמוֹ מִן הַכְּלָל, כָּפַר בָּעִקָּר. וְאַף אַתָּה הַקְהֵה אֶת-שִׁנָּיו, וֶאֱמָר לוֹ: בַּעֲבוּר זֶה, עָשָׂה יְיָ לִי, בְּצֵאתִי מִמִּצְרָיִם, לִי וְלֹא לוֹ. אִלּוּ הָיָה שָׁם, לֹא הָיָה נִגְאָל.

תָּם

THE SIMPLE SON — what does he say? 'What is this?' Tell him: 'God rescued us from slavery in Egypt with a strong hand.'

מַה הוּא אוֹמֵר? מַה זֹּאת? וְאָמַרְתָּ אֵלָיו: בְּחֹזֶק יָד הוֹצִיאָנוּ
יְיָ מִמִּצְרַיִם מִבֵּית עֲבָדִים.

וְשֶׁאֵינוֹ יוֹדֵעַ לִשְׁאֹל

As for **THE SON WHO IS UNABLE TO ASK**, you must start by saying to him, as it says: You should tell your son on that day: 'This is the reason God did so for me when I left Egypt.'

אַתְּ פְּתַח לוֹ. שֶׁנֶּאֱמַר: וְהִגַּדְתָּ לְבִנְךָ, בַּיּוֹם הַהוּא
לֵאמֹר: בַּעֲבוּר זֶה עָשָׂה יְיָ לִי, בְּצֵאתִי מִמִּצְרָיִם.

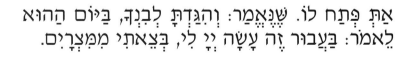

RABBI ISRAEL OF SALANT, THE FOUNDER OF THE MUSSAR MOVEMENT, WHICH STRESSES ETHICAL AND MORAL SELF-IMPROVEMENT, SAID "EVERY PERSON MAY CONTAIN WITHIN HIMSELF ALL THE FOUR SONS."

יָכוֹל מֵרֹאשׁ חֹדֶשׁ, תַּלְמוּד לוֹמַר בַּיּוֹם הַהוּא. אִי בַּיּוֹם הַהוּא. יָכוֹל מִבְּעוֹד יוֹם. תַּלְמוּד לוֹמַר. בַּעֲבוּר זֶה בַּעֲבוּר זֶה לֹא אָמַרְתִּי, אֶלָּא בְּשָׁעָה שֶׁיֵּשׁ מַצָּה וּמָרוֹר מֻנָּחִים לְפָנֶיךָ.

You might think that you need to discuss the Exodus on the first day of the month of Nissan. But the Torah says: 'You should tell your son on that day.' But you can understand the expression 'on that day' to mean only during the daytime; so the Torah adds: 'This is the reason that God did this for me when I went out of Egypt.' 'This' means that it is something you can touch, while the sentence 'You shall tell your son' applies only at the Seder when matzah and maror are at the table.

מִתְּחִלָּה עוֹבְדֵי עֲבוֹדָה זָרָה הָיוּ אֲבוֹתֵינוּ. וְעַכְשָׁו קֵרְבָנוּ הַמָּקוֹם לַעֲבוֹדָתוֹ. שֶׁנֶּאֱמַר: וַיֹּאמֶר יְהוֹשֻׁעַ אֶל כָּל הָעָם. כֹּה אָמַר יְיָ אֱלֹהֵי יִשְׂרָאֵל, בְּעֵבֶר הַנָּהָר יָשְׁבוּ אֲבוֹתֵיכֶם מֵעוֹלָם, תֶּרַח אֲבִי אַבְרָהָם וַאֲבִי נָחוֹר. וַיַּעַבְדוּ אֱלֹהִים אֲחֵרִים. וָאֶקַּח אֶת אֲבִיכֶם אֶת אַבְרָהָם מֵעֵבֶר הַנָּהָר, וָאוֹלֵךְ אוֹתוֹ בְּכָל אֶרֶץ כְּנָעַן וָאַרְבֶּה אֶת זַרְעוֹ, וָאֶתֶּן לוֹ אֶת יִצְחָק. וָאֶתֵּן לְיִצְחָק אֶת יַעֲקֹב וְאֶת עֵשָׂו. וָאֶתֵּן לְעֵשָׂו אֶת הַר שֵׂעִיר, לָרֶשֶׁת אֹתוֹ. וְיַעֲקֹב וּבָנָיו יָרְדוּ מִצְרָיִם.

Originally our ancestors were idol worshipers, but now God made us believers in Him, just as it says: Joshua said to all the people, 'God of Israel says: Your ancestors Terach the father of Abraham and Nachor always lived across the Euphrates River serving other Gods. Then I took your father Abraham from across the river and led him through all the land of Canaan. I gave him a son, Isaac. I gave Isaac, Jacob and Esau; I gave Esau, Mount Seir, but Jacob and his children went down to Egypt.'

בָּרוּךְ שׁוֹמֵר הַבְטָחָתוֹ לְיִשְׂרָאֵל. בָּרוּךְ הוּא. שֶׁהַקָּדוֹשׁ בָּרוּךְ הוּא חִשַּׁב אֶת הַקֵּץ, לַעֲשׂוֹת כְּמָה שֶׁאָמַר לְאַבְרָהָם אָבִינוּ בִּבְרִית בֵּין הַבְּתָרִים. שֶׁנֶּאֱמַר: וַיֹּאמֶר לְאַבְרָם יָדֹעַ תֵּדַע, כִּי גֵר יִהְיֶה זַרְעֲךָ, בְּאֶרֶץ לֹא לָהֶם, וַעֲבָדוּם וְעִנּוּ אֹתָם אַרְבַּע מֵאוֹת שָׁנָה. וְגַם אֶת הַגּוֹי אֲשֶׁר יַעֲבֹדוּ דָּן אָנֹכִי. וְאַחֲרֵי כֵן יֵצְאוּ, בִּרְכֻשׁ גָּדוֹל.

Blessed is He Who keeps His promise to Israel; blessed is He! For the Holy One planned the end of slavery just as He promised to our father Abraham at the Covenant between the Parts, just as it says: He said to Abram, 'Your people will certainly be foreigners in a land that is not theirs, they will be slaves and experience hardship for four hundred years; but I will also act against the people who made them slaves, and afterwards your people will escape with great riches.'

Cover the matzahs, lift the cup, and say.

וְהִיא שֶׁעָמְדָה לַאֲבוֹתֵינוּ וְלָנוּ. שֶׁלֹּא
אֶחָד בִּלְבָד, עָמַד עָלֵינוּ לְכַלּוֹתֵנוּ. אֶלָּא
שֶׁבְּכָל דּוֹר וָדוֹר, עוֹמְדִים עָלֵינוּ לְכַלּוֹתֵנוּ.
וְהַקָּדוֹשׁ בָּרוּךְ הוּא מַצִּילֵנוּ מִיָּדָם.

And this is what has protected our ancestors and us. Because not only one enemy has tried to destroy us, but in every generation, they try and destroy us. But the Holy One rescues us.

Put down the cup and uncover the matzahs.

צֵא וּלְמַד, מַה בִּקֵּשׁ לָבָן הָאֲרַמִּי
לַעֲשׂוֹת לְיַעֲקֹב אָבִינוּ. שֶׁפַּרְעֹה לֹא גָזַר
אֶלָּא עַל הַזְּכָרִים, וְלָבָן בִּקֵּשׁ לַעֲקֹר אֶת
הַכֹּל. שֶׁנֶּאֱמַר:
אֲרַמִּי אֹבֵד אָבִי, וַיֵּרֶד מִצְרַיְמָה,
וַיָּגָר שָׁם בִּמְתֵי מְעָט. וַיְהִי שָׁם לְגוֹי
גָּדוֹל, עָצוּם וָרָב.

Go and learn what Laban the Aramean tried to do to our father Jacob! Though the Pharaoh spoke out against only the males, Laban tried to affect everything, just as it says:
An Aramean tried to kill my father. Then he went down to Egypt and lived there with few people; and there he became a nation — great, mighty, and with many people.

- In Ashkenazic communities, men and women each do their part in baking the matzot.
- In Sephardic communities, the women bake the matzot because they can do it faster. They sing special songs and poems as they work.
- Libyan Jews recite Hallel while baking the matzot, just as the Jews had done during Passover sacrifice preparations throughout Temple times.

In Yemen, the women bake fresh matzah every day.

וַיֵּרֶד מִצְרַיְמָה — אָנוּס עַל פִּי הַדִּבּוּר. **וַיָּגָר שָׁם** — מְלַמֵּד שֶׁלֹּא יָרַד יַעֲקֹב אָבִינוּ לְהִשְׁתַּקֵּעַ בְּמִצְרַיִם, אֶלָּא לָגוּר שָׁם, שֶׁנֶּאֱמַר: וַיֹּאמְרוּ, אֶל פַּרְעֹה, לָגוּר בָּאָרֶץ בָּאנוּ, כִּי אֵין מִרְעֶה לַצֹּאן אֲשֶׁר לַעֲבָדֶיךָ, כִּי כָבֵד הָרָעָב בְּאֶרֶץ כְּנָעַן. וְעַתָּה, יֵשְׁבוּ נָא עֲבָדֶיךָ בְּאֶרֶץ גֹּשֶׁן. **בִּמְתֵי מְעָט** — כְּמָה שֶׁנֶּאֱמַר: בְּשִׁבְעִים נֶפֶשׁ, יָרְדוּ אֲבֹתֶיךָ מִצְרָיְמָה. וְעַתָּה, שָׂמְךָ יְיָ אֱלֹהֶיךָ, כְּכוֹכְבֵי הַשָּׁמַיִם לָרֹב. **וַיְהִי שָׁם לְגוֹי** — מְלַמֵּד שֶׁהָיוּ יִשְׂרָאֵל מְצֻיָּנִים שָׁם. **גָּדוֹל עָצוּם** — כְּמָה שֶׁנֶּאֱמַר: וּבְנֵי יִשְׂרָאֵל, פָּרוּ וַיִּשְׁרְצוּ, וַיִּרְבּוּ וַיַּעַצְמוּ, בִּמְאֹד מְאֹד. וַתִּמָּלֵא הָאָרֶץ אֹתָם.

THEN HE WENT DOWN TO EGYPT — God wanted it that way. **HE LIVED THERE** — this teaches us that Jacob did not go down to Egypt to make a permanent home, but only to live there for a short time, just as it says: The sons of Jacob said to Pharaoh: 'We have come to live in this land because there is no pasture for our flocks, because there is great famine in the land of Canaan. And now, please, let us live in the land of Goshen.' **WITH FEW PEOPLE** — as it is written: With seventy people, your ancestors went down to Egypt, and now your God has made it so that you have as many people as the stars in the sky. **THERE HE BECAME A NATION** — this teaches that the Israelites stood apart as a separate people. **GREAT, MIGHTY** — just as it says: And the children of Israel had many sons and daughters and became very, very mighty; and they filled the land.

Any sign of the Afikoman?

Not a crumb!

She is only omulating the Israelites making mortar for the bricks.

וָרָב — כְּמָה שֶׁנֶּאֱמַר: רְבָבָה כְּצֶמַח הַשָּׂדֶה נְתַתִּיךְ, וַתִּרְבִּי, וַתִּגְדְּלִי, וַתָּבֹאִי בַּעֲדִי עֲדָיִים. שָׁדַיִם נָכֹנוּ, וּשְׂעָרֵךְ צִמֵּחַ, וְאַתְּ עֵרֹם וְעֶרְיָה. וַיָּרֵעוּ אֹתָנוּ הַמִּצְרִים וַיְעַנּוּנוּ. וַיִּתְּנוּ עָלֵינוּ עֲבֹדָה קָשָׁה. וַיָּרֵעוּ אֹתָנוּ הַמִּצְרִים — כְּמָה שֶׁנֶּאֱמַר: הָבָה נִתְחַכְּמָה לוֹ. פֶּן יִרְבֶּה, וְהָיָה כִּי תִקְרֶאנָה מִלְחָמָה, וְנוֹסַף גַּם הוּא עַל שֹׂנְאֵינוּ, וְנִלְחַם בָּנוּ וְעָלָה מִן הָאָרֶץ.

וַיְעַנּוּנוּ — כְּמָה שֶׁנֶּאֱמַר: וַיָּשִׂימוּ עָלָיו שָׂרֵי מִסִּים, לְמַעַן עַנֹּתוֹ בְּסִבְלֹתָם: וַיִּבֶן עָרֵי מִסְכְּנוֹת לְפַרְעֹה, אֶת פִּתֹם וְאֶת רַעַמְסֵס. וַיִּתְּנוּ עָלֵינוּ עֲבֹדָה קָשָׁה — כְּמָה שֶׁנֶּאֱמַר: וַיַּעֲבִדוּ מִצְרַיִם אֶת בְּנֵי יִשְׂרָאֵל בְּפָרֶךְ. וַנִּצְעַק אֶל יְיָ אֱלֹהֵי אֲבֹתֵינוּ, וַיִּשְׁמַע יְיָ אֶת קֹלֵנוּ, וַיַּרְא אֶת עָנְיֵנוּ, וְאֶת עֲמָלֵנוּ, וְאֶת לַחֲצֵנוּ. וַנִּצְעַק אֶל יְיָ אֱלֹהֵי אֲבֹתֵינוּ — כְּמָה שֶׁנֶּאֱמַר: וַיְהִי בַיָּמִים הָרַבִּים הָהֵם, וַיָּמָת מֶלֶךְ מִצְרַיִם, וַיֵּאָנְחוּ בְנֵי יִשְׂרָאֵל מִן הָעֲבֹדָה וַיִּזְעָקוּ. וַתַּעַל שַׁוְעָתָם אֶל הָאֱלֹהִים מִן הָעֲבֹדָה. וַיִּשְׁמַע יְיָ אֶת קֹלֵנוּ — כְּמָה שֶׁנֶּאֱמַר: וַיִּשְׁמַע אֱלֹהִים אֶת נַאֲקָתָם. וַיִּזְכֹּר אֱלֹהִים אֶת בְּרִיתוֹ, אֶת אַבְרָהָם, אֶת יִצְחָק, וְאֶת יַעֲקֹב.

MANY — just as it says: I made you as many as there are plants of the field;you grew and became charming and with a beautiful figure; your hair grown long; but, you were naked and bare. And I looked at you and saw you on the ground in your blood and I said to you: 'Through your blood shall you live!' And I said to you: 'Through your blood shall you live!'.The Egyptians did evil to us and harmed us; and made us work hard. The Egyptians did evil to us — just as it says: Let us be smart about dealing with them or else they will continue to have children and if we happen to be at war, they may join our enemies and fight against us and then leave the country. And harmed us — just as it says: They watched over us and made us work hard; and they made us build Pithom and Raamses as special cities for Pharaoh.They made us do hard work — just as it says: The Egyptians overwhelmed the children of Israel with hard work. We cried out to God, the God of our fathers; and He heard our cry and saw our hardship, our burden, and our grief. We cried out to God, the God of our fathers — just as it says in: During that time, the king of Egypt died; and the children of Israel groaned because of their slavery, and cried; and God heard their cry.' God heard our cry — just as it says: God heard their groaning, and God remembered His agreement with Abraham, with Isaac, and with Jacob.

וַיַּרְא אֶת עָנְיֵנוּ — זוֹ פְּרִישׁוּת דֶּרֶךְ
אֶרֶץ. כְּמָה שֶׁנֶּאֱמַר: וַיַּרְא אֱלֹהִים אֶת בְּנֵי
יִשְׂרָאֵל. וַיֵּדַע אֱלֹהִים. וְאֶת עֲמָלֵנוּ —
אֵלּוּ הַבָּנִים. כְּמָה שֶׁנֶּאֱמַר: כָּל הַבֵּן הַיִּלּוֹד
הַיְאֹרָה תַּשְׁלִיכֻהוּ, וְכָל הַבַּת תְּחַיּוּן. וְאֶת
לַחֲצֵנוּ — זֶה הַדְּחַק. כְּמָה שֶׁנֶּאֱמַר: וְגַם
רָאִיתִי אֶת הַלַּחַץ, אֲשֶׁר מִצְרַיִם לֹחֲצִים
אֹתָם. וַיּוֹצִאֵנוּ יְיָ מִמִּצְרַיִם, בְּיָד חֲזָקָה, וּבִזְרֹעַ
נְטוּיָה, וּבְמֹרָא גָּדֹל וּבְאֹתוֹת וּבְמֹפְתִים.
וַיּוֹצִאֵנוּ יְיָ מִמִּצְרַיִם — לֹא עַל יְדֵי
מַלְאָךְ, וְלֹא עַל יְדֵי שָׂרָף. וְלֹא עַל יְדֵי שָׁלִיחַ.
אֶלָּא הַקָּדוֹשׁ בָּרוּךְ הוּא בִּכְבוֹדוֹ וּבְעַצְמוֹ.
שֶׁנֶּאֱמַר: וְעָבַרְתִּי בְאֶרֶץ מִצְרַיִם בַּלַּיְלָה הַזֶּה,
וְהִכֵּיתִי כָל בְּכוֹר בְּאֶרֶץ מִצְרַיִם, מֵאָדָם וְעַד
בְּהֵמָה, וּבְכָל אֱלֹהֵי מִצְרַיִם אֶעֱשֶׂה שְׁפָטִים
אֲנִי יְיָ. וְעָבַרְתִּי בְאֶרֶץ מִצְרַיִם בַּלַּיְלָה הַזֶּה
— אֲנִי וְלֹא מַלְאָךְ. וְהִכֵּיתִי כָל בְּכוֹר בְּאֶרֶץ
מִצְרַיִם. אֲנִי וְלֹא שָׂרָף. וּבְכָל אֱלֹהֵי מִצְרַיִם
אֶעֱשֶׂה שְׁפָטִים — אֲנִי וְלֹא הַשָּׁלִיחַ.
אֲנִי יְיָ — אֲנִי הוּא וְלֹא אַחֵר. בְּיָד חֲזָקָה.
זוֹ הַדֶּבֶר. כְּמָה שֶׁנֶּאֱמַר: הִנֵּה יַד יְיָ הוֹיָה,
בְּמִקְנְךָ אֲשֶׁר בַּשָּׂדֶה, בַּסּוּסִים בַּחֲמֹרִים
בַּגְּמַלִּים, בַּבָּקָר וּבַצֹּאן, דֶּבֶר כָּבֵד מְאֹד.

• The Haggadah first appeared in the Mishnah in 200 C.E.
It has been translated into more than 20 languages, with the first English version written in 1794.
There are more than 3,000 known published editions of the Pesach Haggadah.

Why print a new Haggadah every year? Because it gives last year's wicked son a chance to become a tzadik!

And saw our hardship — that is how it ruined family life, just as it says: God saw the children of Israel and God took note. **Our grief** — means the children, just as it says: Every one of your newborn sons will be cast into the river, but every daughter will live. **Our hardship** — means the evil way the Egyptians spoke to them, just as it says: I have also seen how the Egyptians are making them suffer. **God rescued us from Egypt with a mighty hand and an outstretched arm, with great awe, with signs and with wonders. God rescued us from Egypt** — an angel didn't rescue us, or a spirit, or a messenger, but only the Holy One in His glory, just as it says: I will pass through the land of Egypt on that night; I will slay all the firstborn in the land of Egypt, both man and animal; and I will act against all the gods of Egypt. 'I will pass through the land of Egypt on that night' — I and not an angel; 'I will slay all the firstborn in the land of Egypt' — I and not a spirit; 'And I will act against all the gods of Egypt' — I and not a messenger; 'I, God' — it is I and no other. **With a mighty hand** — means the disease, just as it says: Beware, God's hand will strike your cattle which are in the field, the horses, the donkeys, the camels, the herds, and the flocks — a very serious disease.

וּבִזְרֹעַ נְטוּיָה – זוֹ הַחֶרֶב. כְּמָה שֶׁנֶּאֱמַר: וְחַרְבּוֹ שְׁלוּפָה בְּיָדוֹ, נְטוּיָה עַל יְרוּשָׁלָיִם. וּבְמֹרָא גָּדֹל – זֶה גִּלּוּי שְׁכִינָה. כְּמָה שֶׁנֶּאֱמַר: אוֹ הֲנִסָּה אֱלֹהִים, לָבוֹא לָקַחַת לוֹ גוֹי מִקֶּרֶב גּוֹי, בְּמַסֹּת בְּאֹתֹת וּבְמוֹפְתִים וּבְמִלְחָמָה, וּבְיָד חֲזָקָה וּבִזְרוֹעַ נְטוּיָה, וּבְמוֹרָאִים גְּדֹלִים. כְּכֹל אֲשֶׁר עָשָׂה לָכֶם יְיָ אֱלֹהֵיכֶם בְּמִצְרַיִם, לְעֵינֶיךָ. וּבְאֹתוֹת – זֶה הַמַּטֶּה. כְּמָה שֶׁנֶּאֱמַר: וְאֶת הַמַּטֶּה הַזֶּה תִּקַּח בְּיָדֶךָ. אֲשֶׁר תַּעֲשֶׂה בּוֹ אֶת הָאֹתֹת. וּבְמוֹפְתִים – זֶה הַדָּם. כְּמָה שֶׁנֶּאֱמַר: וְנָתַתִּי מוֹפְתִים, בַּשָּׁמַיִם וּבָאָרֶץ:

With an outstretched arm — means the sword, just as it says: The sword in his hand, outstretched over Jerusalem. **With great awe** — hints at the appearance of the Spirit, just as it says: Has God ever tried to take a nation from another nation by challenges, miraculous signs, and wonders, with a mighty hand and outstretched arm and by incredible happenings, just as your God has done for you in Egypt, right in front of you? **With signs** — means the miracles created with the staff, just as it says: Take this staff in your hand so that you can make miracles with it. **With wonders** — hints at the blood, just as it says: I will show wonders in the heavens and on the earth:

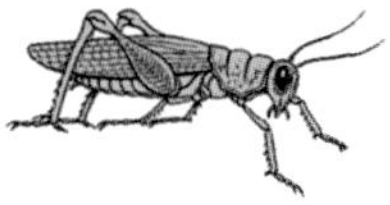

For each of the words, spill a drop of wine:

דָּם, וָאֵשׁ, וְתִימְרוֹת עָשָׁן.

Blood, Fire, and Pillars of Smoke.

דָּבָר אַחֵר. בְּיָד חֲזָקָה – שְׁתַּיִם. וּבִזְרֹעַ נְטוּיָה שְׁתַּיִם. וּבְמֹרָא גָּדוֹל – שְׁתַּיִם.
וּבְאֹתוֹת – שְׁתַּיִם. וּבְמֹפְתִים – שְׁתַּיִם.
אֵלּוּ עֶשֶׂר מַכּוֹת שֶׁהֵבִיא הַקָּדוֹשׁ בָּרוּךְ הוּא עַל הַמִּצְרִים בְּמִצְרַיִם, וְאֵלּוּ הֵן.

Each group of words might also stand for two plagues. For example: **Mighty hand** — two; **outstretched arm** — two; **great awe** — two; **signs** — two; **wonders** — two.
These are the ten plagues which God brought upon the Egyptians in Egypt, and they are:

Spill a drop of wine as each plague is mentioned.

THE TEN PLAGUES

1 **BLOOD**	דָּם 1
2 **FROGS**	צְפַרְדֵּעַ 2
3 **VERMIN**	כִּנִּים 3
4 **WILD BEASTS**	עָרוֹב 4
5 **CATTLE DISEASE**	דֶּבֶר 5
6 **BOILS**	שְׁחִין 6
7 **HAIL**	בָּרָד 7
8 **LOCUSTS**	אַרְבֶּה 8
9 **DARKNESS**	חֹשֶׁךְ 9
10 **PLAGUE OF THE FIRSTBORN.**	מַכַּת בְּכוֹרוֹת 10

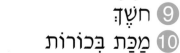

LAGUES
1
Bogus, dudes!
2
Me 'n' da boys, we're takin' over, see?
3
LICE!..LICE! we got LICE!
SKRITCH
SKRATCH
4
You think you saw WHAT!?
FOAM
5
We get a lot of that this time of year!

THE TEN
WHO told you zits turn into boils on Passover?
6
7
YES, Locust may be kosher. NO, you may not feed a grasshopper to your sister!
8
So... how d'you like being the oldest NOW, big shot?
9
Errr... about that electric biLL, Pharaoh...
10

רַבִּי יְהוּדָה

הָיָה נוֹתֵן בָּהֶם סִמָּנִים:

דְּצַ״ךְ עֲדַ״שׁ בְּאַחַ״ב

רַבִּי יוֹסֵי הַגְּלִילִי אוֹמֵר

מִנַּיִן אַתָּה אוֹמֵר, שֶׁלָּקוּ הַמִּצְרִים בְּמִצְרַיִם עֶשֶׂר מַכּוֹת, וְעַל הַיָּם, לָקוּ חֲמִשִּׁים מַכּוֹת? בְּמִצְרַיִם מַה הוּא אוֹמֵר? וַיֹּאמְרוּ הַחַרְטֻמִּם אֶל פַּרְעֹה, אֶצְבַּע אֱלֹהִים הִוא. וְעַל הַיָּם מַה הוּא אוֹמֵר? וַיַּרְא יִשְׂרָאֵל אֶת הַיָּד הַגְּדֹלָה, אֲשֶׁר עָשָׂה יְיָ בְּמִצְרַיִם, וַיִּירְאוּ הָעָם אֶת יְיָ. וַיַּאֲמִינוּ בַּיְיָ, וּבְמשֶׁה עַבְדּוֹ. כַּמָּה לָקוּ בְאֶצְבַּע? עֶשֶׂר מַכּוֹת. אֱמוֹר מֵעַתָּה, בְּמִצְרַיִם לָקוּ עֶשֶׂר מַכּוֹת, וְעַל הַיָּם, לָקוּ חֲמִשִּׁים מַכּוֹת:

רַבִּי אֱלִיעֶזֶר אוֹמֵר

מִנַּיִן שֶׁכָּל מַכָּה וּמַכָּה, שֶׁהֵבִיא הַקָּדוֹשׁ בָּרוּךְ הוּא עַל הַמִּצְרִים בְּמִצְרַיִם, הָיְתָה שֶׁל אַרְבַּע מַכּוֹת? שֶׁנֶּאֱמַר: יְשַׁלַּח בָּם חֲרוֹן אַפּוֹ, עֶבְרָה וָזַעַם וְצָרָה. מִשְׁלַחַת מַלְאֲכֵי רָעִים. עֶבְרָה — אַחַת. וָזַעַם — שְׁתַּיִם. וְצָרָה — שָׁלֹשׁ. מִשְׁלַחַת מַלְאֲכֵי רָעִים — אַרְבַּע. אֱמוֹר מֵעַתָּה: בְּמִצְרַיִם לָקוּ אַרְבָּעִים מַכּוֹת, וְעַל הַיָּם לָקוּ מָאתַיִם מַכּוֹת.

רַבִּי עֲקִיבָא אוֹמֵר

מִנַּיִן שֶׁכָּל מַכָּה וּמַכָּה שֶׁהֵבִיא הַקָּדוֹשׁ בָּרוּךְ הוּא עַל הַמִּצְרִים בְּמִצְרַיִם, הָיְתָה שֶׁל חָמֵשׁ מַכּוֹת? שֶׁנֶּאֱמַר: יְשַׁלַּח בָּם חֲרוֹן אַפּוֹ, עֶבְרָה וָזַעַם וְצָרָה. מִשְׁלַחַת מַלְאֲכֵי רָעִים. חֲרוֹן אַפּוֹ — אַחַת, עֶבְרָה — שְׁתַּיִם, וָזַעַם - שָׁלֹשׁ, וְצָרָה — אַרְבַּע, מִשְׁלַחַת מַלְאֲכֵי רָעִים — חָמֵשׁ. אֱמוֹר מֵעַתָּה, בְּמִצְרַיִם לָקוּ חֲמִשִּׁים מַכּוֹת, וְעַל הַיָּם לָקוּ חֲמִשִּׁים וּמָאתַיִם מַכּוֹת.

Rabbi Judah abbreviated them using their Hebrew Initials:

D'TZACH, ADASH, B'ACHAB

Rabbi Yose the Galilean said How do we know that the Egyptians were struck with ten plagues in Egypt and fifty plagues at the Sea? — The Torah says about the plagues in Egypt (Exodus 8:15): The magicians said to Pharaoh, 'It is the finger of God.' However, of those at the Sea, the Torah tells (Exodus 14:31): Israel saw the great 'hand' which GOD put on the Egyptians, the people feared GOD and they believed in God and in His servant Moses. How many plagues did they receive with the finger? Ten! Then if they suffered ten plagues in Egypt (where they were struck with a finger), they must have been made to suffer fifty plagues at the Sea (where they were struck with a whole hand).

Rabbi Eliezer said How do we know that every plague that God put on the Egyptians in Egypt was equal to four plagues? — Because it says in Psalms 78:49: He sent on them His fierce anger: Rage, fury, trouble, and a gang of evil-doers. (Since each plague in Egypt was made up of) 1) rage, 2) fury, 3) trouble and 4) a gang of evil-doers, they must have been struck by forty plagues in Egypt and by two hundred at the Sea!

Rabbi Akiva said How do we know that each plague that God put on the Egyptians in Egypt was equal to five plagues? — Because it is written: He sent His fierce anger on them, rage, fury, trouble, and a gang of evil-doers. (Since in each plague in Egypt there was: 1) fierce anger, 2) rage, 3) fury, 4) trouble, and 5) a gang of evil-doers, they must have been struck by fifty plagues in Egypt and by two hundred and fifty at the sea!

כַּמָּה מַעֲלוֹת טוֹבוֹת לַמָּקוֹם עָלֵינוּ!

אִלּוּ הוֹצִיאָנוּ מִמִּצְרַיִם, וְלֹא עָשָׂה בָהֶם שְׁפָטִים, דַּיֵּנוּ!
אִלּוּ עָשָׂה בָהֶם שְׁפָטִים, וְלֹא עָשָׂה בֵאלֹהֵיהֶם, דַּיֵּנוּ!
אִלּוּ עָשָׂה בֵאלֹהֵיהֶם, וְלֹא הָרַג אֶת בְּכוֹרֵיהֶם, דַּיֵּנוּ!
אִלּוּ הָרַג אֶת בְּכוֹרֵיהֶם, וְלֹא נָתַן לָנוּ אֶת מָמוֹנָם, דַּיֵּנוּ!
אִלּוּ נָתַן לָנוּ אֶת מָמוֹנָם, וְלֹא קָרַע לָנוּ אֶת הַיָּם, דַּיֵּנוּ!
אִלּוּ קָרַע לָנוּ אֶת הַיָּם, וְלֹא הֶעֱבִירָנוּ בְתוֹכוֹ בֶּחָרָבָה, דַּיֵּנוּ!
אִלּוּ הֶעֱבִירָנוּ בְתוֹכוֹ בֶּחָרָבָה, וְלֹא שִׁקַּע צָרֵינוּ בְּתוֹכוֹ, דַּיֵּנוּ!
אִלּוּ שִׁקַּע צָרֵינוּ בְּתוֹכוֹ, וְלֹא סִפֵּק צָרְכֵּנוּ בַּמִּדְבָּר אַרְבָּעִים שָׁנָה, דַּיֵּנוּ!
אִלּוּ סִפֵּק צָרְכֵּנוּ בַּמִּדְבָּר אַרְבָּעִים שָׁנָה, וְלֹא הֶאֱכִילָנוּ אֶת הַמָּן, דַּיֵּנוּ!
אִלּוּ הֶאֱכִילָנוּ אֶת הַמָּן, וְלֹא נָתַן לָנוּ אֶת הַשַּׁבָּת, דַּיֵּנוּ!
אִלּוּ נָתַן לָנוּ אֶת הַשַּׁבָּת, וְלֹא קֵרְבָנוּ לִפְנֵי הַר סִינַי, דַּיֵּנוּ!
אִלּוּ קֵרְבָנוּ לִפְנֵי הַר סִינַי, וְלֹא נָתַן לָנוּ אֶת הַתּוֹרָה, דַּיֵּנוּ!
אִלּוּ נָתַן לָנוּ אֶת הַתּוֹרָה, וְלֹא הִכְנִיסָנוּ לְאֶרֶץ יִשְׂרָאֵל, דַּיֵּנוּ!
אִלּוּ הִכְנִיסָנוּ לְאֶרֶץ יִשְׂרָאֵל, וְלֹא בָנָה לָנוּ אֶת בֵּית הַבְּחִירָה, דַּיֵּנוּ!

עַל אַחַת כַּמָּה וְכַמָּה טוֹבָה כְפוּלָה וּמְכֻפֶּלֶת לַמָּקוֹם עָלֵינוּ:

שֶׁהוֹצִיאָנוּ מִמִּצְרַיִם,
וְעָשָׂה בָהֶם שְׁפָטִים,
וְעָשָׂה בֵאלֹהֵיהֶם,
וְהָרַג אֶת בְּכוֹרֵיהֶם,
וְנָתַן לָנוּ אֶת מָמוֹנָם,
וְקָרַע לָנוּ אֶת הַיָּם,
וְהֶעֱבִירָנוּ בְתוֹכוֹ בֶּחָרָבָה,
וְשִׁקַּע צָרֵינוּ בְּתוֹכוֹ,
וְסִפֵּק צָרְכֵּנוּ בַּמִּדְבָּר אַרְבָּעִים שָׁנָה,
וְהֶאֱכִילָנוּ אֶת הַמָּן,
וְנָתַן לָנוּ אֶת הַשַּׁבָּת,
וְקֵרְבָנוּ לִפְנֵי הַר סִינַי,
וְנָתַן לָנוּ אֶת הַתּוֹרָה,
וְהִכְנִיסָנוּ לְאֶרֶץ יִשְׂרָאֵל,
וּבָנָה לָנוּ אֶת בֵּית הַבְּחִירָה
לְכַפֵּר עַל כָּל עֲוֹנוֹתֵינוּ.

Don't even think about it!

DARN! Almost had her!!!

How many are the good deeds that the Eternal has done for us!

Had He rescued us from Egypt, but did nothing against the Egyptians,
it would have been enough for us!
Had He acted against them, but not against their Gods...enough!
Had He acted against their Gods, but not killed their firstborn...enough!
Had He killed their firstborn, but not given us their riches...enough!
Had He given us their riches but not split the Sea for us...enough!
Had he split the Sea for us, but not led us through it on dry land...enough!
Had He led us through it on dry land, but not drowned our enemies in it...enough!
Had he drowned our enemies in it, but not cared for us in the desert for forty years ...enough!
Had He taken care of us in the desert for forty years, but not fed us the Manna ...enough!
Had He fed us the Manna, but not given us the Sabbath...enough!
Had He given us the Sabbath, but not brought us to Mount Sinai...enough!
Had He given us the Torah, but not brought us into the Land of Israel...enough!
Had He brought us into the Land of Israel, but not built the Temple for us,
it would have been enough for us!

So, how much more should we be thankful to God for all the many things He has done for us: He rescued us from Egypt; acted against the Egyptians; and against their Gods; killed their firstborn; gave us their riches; split the Sea for us; led us through it on dry land; drowned our enemies in it; took care of us in the desert for forty years; fed us the Manna; gave us the Sabbath; brought us before Mount Sinai; gave us the Torah; brought us to the Land of Israel; and built us the Temple to ask forgiveness for all our sins.

Wow, Mom! The table's set so beautifully—even if you didn't cook this delicious meal, it would have been enough for me!
Why, thank you, Oody!
Had you cooked this delicious meal , and didn't bake this amazing chocolate layer matzah cake , it would have been enough for me!
Er... thank you, Oody!
Had you baked this amazing chocolate layer matzah cake ... Oh, by the way, could I have a small...

Rabban Gamliel used to say: Whoever has not explained the following three things on Passover has not fulfilled his duty: **PASSOVER SACRIFICE** , **MATZAH** and **BITTER HERBS**.

רַבָּן גַּמְלִיאֵל הָיָה אוֹמֵר: כָּל שֶׁלֹּא אָמַר שְׁלֹשָׁה דְבָרִים אֵלּוּ בַּפֶּסַח, לֹא יָצָא יְדֵי חוֹבָתוֹ, וְאֵלּוּ הֵן:

פֶּסַח • מַצָּה • וּמָרוֹר

The leader points to the Matzah and Maror when they are mentioned:

פֶּסַח שֶׁהָיוּ אֲבוֹתֵינוּ אוֹכְלִים, בִּזְמַן שֶׁבֵּית הַמִּקְדָּשׁ הָיָה קַיָּם, עַל שׁוּם מָה? — עַל שׁוּם שֶׁפָּסַח הַקָּדוֹשׁ בָּרוּךְ הוּא, עַל בָּתֵּי אֲבוֹתֵינוּ בְּמִצְרַיִם, שֶׁנֶּאֱמַר: וַאֲמַרְתֶּם זֶבַח פֶּסַח הוּא לַייָ, אֲשֶׁר פָּסַח עַל בָּתֵּי בְנֵי יִשְׂרָאֵל בְּמִצְרַיִם, בְּנָגְפּוֹ אֶת מִצְרַיִם וְאֶת בָּתֵּינוּ הִצִּיל, וַיִּקֹּד הָעָם וַיִּשְׁתַּחֲווּ. מַצָּה זוֹ שֶׁאָנוּ אוֹכְלִים, עַל שׁוּם מָה? — עַל שׁוּם שֶׁלֹּא הִסְפִּיק בְּצֵקָם שֶׁל אֲבוֹתֵינוּ לְהַחֲמִיץ, עַד שֶׁנִּגְלָה עֲלֵיהֶם מֶלֶךְ מַלְכֵי הַמְּלָכִים, הַקָּדוֹשׁ בָּרוּךְ הוּא, וּגְאָלָם, שֶׁנֶּאֱמַר: וַיֹּאפוּ אֶת הַבָּצֵק, אֲשֶׁר הוֹצִיאוּ מִמִּצְרַיִם, עֻגֹת מַצּוֹת, כִּי לֹא חָמֵץ; כִּי גֹרְשׁוּ מִמִּצְרַיִם, וְלֹא יָכְלוּ לְהִתְמַהְמֵהַּ, וְגַם צֵדָה לֹא עָשׂוּ לָהֶם. מָרוֹר זֶה שֶׁאָנוּ אוֹכְלִים, עַל שׁוּם מָה? — עַל שׁוּם שֶׁמֵּרְרוּ הַמִּצְרִים אֶת חַיֵּי אֲבוֹתֵינוּ בְּמִצְרַיִם, שֶׁנֶּאֱמַר: וַיְמָרְרוּ אֶת חַיֵּיהֶם בַּעֲבֹדָה בַּשָּׂדֶה; אֶת כָּל עֲבֹדָתָם, אֲשֶׁר עָבְדוּ בָהֶם בְּפָרֶךְ.

On all other nights it is not polite to point. On this night, why do we point twice?

PESACH — Why did our ancestors eat a Passover offering during the time when the Temple still stood? — Because God passed over the houses of our ancestors in Egypt, as it says: You should say: 'It is a Passover offering for God, Who passed over the houses of the children of Israel in Egypt when He struck the Egyptians and saved our houses; and the people bowed down.'

Point to the Matzah and say:

MATZAH — Why do we eat this unleavened bread? — Because the dough of our ancestors did not have time to rise before God came and rescued them, as it says: They baked the dough which they brought out of Egypt into unleavened bread, because it did not rise, because they were quickly chased out of Egypt, and they had not prepared any food for the way.

Point to the Maror and say:

MAROR — Why do we eat this bitter herb? — Because the Egyptians made our ancestors' lives in Egypt hard, as it says: They made their lives difficult with hard labor, with mortar and bricks, and with all kinds of work in the field: whatever service they made them do was with hard labor.

You *definitely* pointed at *me* when you said Maror!

בְּכָל דּוֹר וָדוֹר חַיָּב אָדָם לִרְאוֹת אֶת עַצְמוֹ, כְּאִלּוּ הוּא יָצָא מִמִּצְרָיִם, שֶׁנֶּאֱמַר: וְהִגַּדְתָּ לְבִנְךָ בַּיּוֹם הַהוּא לֵאמֹר: בַּעֲבוּר זֶה עָשָׂה יְיָ לִי, בְּצֵאתִי מִמִּצְרָיִם. לֹא אֶת אֲבוֹתֵינוּ בִּלְבָד, גָּאַל הַקָּדוֹשׁ בָּרוּךְ הוּא, אֶלָּא אַף אוֹתָנוּ גָּאַל עִמָּהֶם, שֶׁנֶּאֱמַר: וְאוֹתָנוּ הוֹצִיא מִשָּׁם, לְמַעַן הָבִיא אֹתָנוּ, לָתֶת לָנוּ אֶת הָאָרֶץ אֲשֶׁר נִשְׁבַּע לַאֲבֹתֵינוּ.

Cover the matzos, lift the cup and say:

לְפִיכָךְ אֲנַחְנוּ חַיָּבִים לְהוֹדוֹת, לְהַלֵּל, לְשַׁבֵּחַ, לְפָאֵר, לְרוֹמֵם, לְהַדֵּר, לְבָרֵךְ, לְעַלֵּה וּלְקַלֵּס, לְמִי שֶׁעָשָׂה לַאֲבוֹתֵינוּ וְלָנוּ אֶת כָּל הַנִּסִּים הָאֵלֶּה. הוֹצִיאָנוּ מֵעַבְדוּת לְחֵרוּת, מִיָּגוֹן לְשִׂמְחָה, מֵאֵבֶל לְיוֹם טוֹב, וּמֵאֲפֵלָה לְאוֹר גָּדוֹל, וּמִשִּׁעְבּוּד לִגְאֻלָּה. וְנֹאמַר לְפָנָיו שִׁירָה חֲדָשָׁה. הַלְלוּיָהּ!

Put the cup down.

הַלְלוּיָהּ! הַלְלוּ עַבְדֵי יְיָ. הַלְלוּ אֶת-שֵׁם יְיָ. יְהִי שֵׁם יְיָ מְבֹרָךְ מֵעַתָּה וְעַד עוֹלָם. מִמִּזְרַח שֶׁמֶשׁ עַד מְבוֹאוֹ. מְהֻלָּל שֵׁם יְיָ. רָם עַל כָּל גּוֹיִם יְיָ. עַל הַשָּׁמַיִם כְּבוֹדוֹ. מִי כַּיְיָ אֱלֹהֵינוּ. הַמַּגְבִּיהִי לָשָׁבֶת. הַמַּשְׁפִּילִי לִרְאוֹת בַּשָּׁמַיִם וּבָאָרֶץ? מְקִימִי מֵעָפָר דָּל. מֵאַשְׁפֹּת יָרִים אֶבְיוֹן. לְהוֹשִׁיבִי עִם נְדִיבִים. עִם נְדִיבֵי עַמּוֹ. מוֹשִׁיבִי עֲקֶרֶת הַבַּיִת אֵם הַבָּנִים שְׂמֵחָה. הַלְלוּיָהּ!

In every generation one must feel as though he personally had been rescued from Egypt, just as it says: You should tell your son on that day: 'It was because of what God did for "me" that I was rescued from Egypt.' God didn't only rescue our ancestors from slavery, but we too, were rescued with them. He brought "us" out from there so that He might take us to the land which He had promised to our ancestors.

Cover the matzos, lift the cup and say:

So it is our duty to thank, praise, applaud, glorify, honor, bless, compliment, and recognize Him, the one Who created all these miracles for our ancestors and for us. He brought us from slavery to freedom, from suffering to joy, from mourning to festivity, from darkness to great light, and from slavery to freedom. Let us sing a new song before Him! Halleluyah!

Put the cup down.

Halleluyah! Praise, you servants of God, praise the Name of God. Blessed be the Name of God from now and forever. God's Name is praised from when the sun rises to when it sets. God is high above all nations and His glory is above the heavens. Who is like our God, Who sits on a high throne and oversees heaven and earth? He raises the poor from the dust, He lifts the needy from the garbage — and seats them with nobles, with the nobles of His people. He changes the wife who can't have children into a happy mother of children. Halleluyah!

בְּצֵאת יִשְׂרָאֵל מִמִּצְרָיִם, בֵּית יַעֲקֹב מֵעַם לֹעֵז, הָיְתָה יְהוּדָה לְקָדְשׁוֹ, יִשְׂרָאֵל מַמְשְׁלוֹתָיו. הַיָּם רָאָה וַיָּנֹס, הַיַּרְדֵּן יִסֹּב לְאָחוֹר. הֶהָרִים רָקְדוּ כְאֵילִים, גְּבָעוֹת — כִּבְנֵי צֹאן. מַה לְּךָ הַיָּם כִּי תָנוּס; הַיַּרְדֵּן תִּסֹּב לְאָחוֹר; הֶהָרִים תִּרְקְדוּ כְאֵילִים; גְּבָעוֹת — כִּבְנֵי צֹאן? מִלִּפְנֵי אָדוֹן חוּלִי אָרֶץ, מִלִּפְנֵי אֱלוֹהַּ יַעֲקֹב. הַהֹפְכִי הַצּוּר אֲגַם מָיִם, חַלָּמִישׁ לְמַעְיְנוֹ-מָיִם.

Lift the cup and say:

בָּרוּךְ אַתָּה יְיָ, אֱלֹהֵינוּ מֶלֶךְ הָעוֹלָם, אֲשֶׁר גְּאָלָנוּ וְגָאַל אֶת-אֲבוֹתֵינוּ מִמִּצְרַיִם, וְהִגִּיעָנוּ לַלַּיְלָה הַזֶּה, לֶאֱכָל-בּוֹ מַצָּה וּמָרוֹר. כֵּן, יְיָ אֱלֹהֵינוּ וֵאלֹהֵי אֲבוֹתֵינוּ, יַגִּיעֵנוּ לְמוֹעֲדִים וְלִרְגָלִים אֲחֵרִים, הַבָּאִים לִקְרָאתֵנוּ לְשָׁלוֹם. שְׂמֵחִים בְּבִנְיַן עִירֶךָ, וְשָׂשִׂים בַּעֲבוֹדָתֶךָ, וְנֹאכַל שָׁם מִן הַזְּבָחִים וּמִן הַפְּסָחִים, אֲשֶׁר יַגִּיעַ דָּמָם, עַל קִיר מִזְבַּחֲךָ לְרָצוֹן, וְנוֹדֶה לְּךָ שִׁיר חָדָשׁ עַל גְּאֻלָּתֵנוּ, וְעַל פְּדוּת נַפְשֵׁנוּ. בָּרוּךְ אַתָּה יְיָ, גָּאַל יִשְׂרָאֵל.

When Israel left Egypt, Jacob's home among foreign people, Israel became His retreat, Israel the place where He ruled. The Sea saw and ran away; the Jordan turned backward. The mountains skipped like rams, and the hills like young lambs. What troubles you, Sea, that you run away? Jordan, that you turn backward? Mountains, that you skip like rams? Hills, like young lambs? In front of God — tremble, earth, in front of the God of Jacob, Who turns the rock into a pond of water, the stone into a flowing fountain.

Lift the cup and say: Blessed are You, our God, King of the universe, Who rescued us and rescued our ancestors from Egypt so that we could be here tonight and eat matzah and maror. So, God and God of our ancestors, also let us enjoy future festivals and holidays in peace, happy that we are rebuilding Your city, and joyful to serve You. At that time, we will eat the Passover sacrifices whose blood is on the sides of Your altar waiting for you to accept them. We will then sing a new song of praise to You for our rescue and for the freedom of our souls. Blessed are You, God, Who has rescued Israel.

בָּרוּךְ אַתָּה יְיָ, אֱלֹהֵינוּ מֶלֶךְ הָעוֹלָם, בּוֹרֵא פְּרִי הַגָּפֶן.

Blessed are You, God, King of the universe, Who creates the fruit of the vine.

Drink the second cup.

ThankyouThankyouThankyouThankyou
Wash your hands and say the blessing – we'll be eating soon

רָחְצָה

WASHING HANDS

בָּרוּךְ אַתָּה יְיָ אֱלֹהֵינוּ מֶלֶךְ הָעוֹלָם אֲשֶׁר קִדְּשָׁנוּ בְּמִצְוֹתָיו וְצִוָּנוּ עַל נְטִילַת יָדָיִם.

Blessed are You, God, King of the universe, Who has honored us with His commandments, and has commanded us to wash our hands.

Say the first blessing over matzah as bread, and the second for the mitzvah of eating matzah:

מוֹצִיא

MOTZI

בָּרוּךְ אַתָּה יְיָ, אֱלֹהֵינוּ מֶלֶךְ הָעוֹלָם,
הַמּוֹצִיא לֶחֶם מִן הָאָרֶץ.

Blessed are You, God, King of the universe, Who makes bread from the earth.

Raise the top matzah and the middle piece, and say:

מַצָּה

MATZAH

בָּרוּךְ אַתָּה יְיָ, אֱלֹהֵינוּ מֶלֶךְ הָעוֹלָם, אֲשֶׁר
קִדְּשָׁנוּ בְּמִצְוֹתָיו וְצִוָּנוּ עַל אֲכִילַת מַצָּה.

Blessed are You, God, King of the universe, Who has honored us with His commandments, and has commanded us to eat matzah.

מָרוֹר

BITTER HERBS

Eat Maror with charoset.

בָּרוּךְ אַתָּה יְיָ, אֱלֹהֵינוּ מֶלֶךְ
הָעוֹלָם, אֲשֶׁר קִדְּשָׁנוּ בְּמִצְוֹתָיו
וְצִוָּנוּ עַל אֲכִילַת מָרוֹר.

Blessed are You, God, King of the universe, Who has honored us with His commandments, and has commanded us to eat Maror.

Used real mortar, didn't you?

כּוֹרֵךְ

BITTER HERBS AND MATZAH

Break the bottom matzah, put maror between two pieces, and say:

זֵכֶר לְמִקְדָּשׁ כְּהִלֵּל.
כֵּן עָשָׂה הִלֵּל בִּזְמַן שֶׁבֵּית
הַמִּקְדָּשׁ הָיָה קַיָּם: הָיָה
כּוֹרֵךְ מַצָּה וּמָרוֹר וְאוֹכֵל
בְּיַחַד. לְקַיֵּם מַה שֶּׁנֶּאֱמַר: עַל
מַצּוֹת וּמְרוֹרִים יֹאכְלֻהוּ.

To remember the Temple, we do as Hillel did: combine matzah and maror and eat them together, just as it is said: They should eat it with matzos and bitter herbs.

שֻׁלְחָן עוֹרֵךְ

FESTIVAL M•E•A•L

UH-OH!..
Nope...
Not here, either...
HOW COULD YOU FORGET WHERE YOU HID THE AFIKOMAN !?!

FIND THE AFIKOMAN

צָפוּן

After the meal, eat a piece of the Afikoman. There is no more eating after this.

Fill the third cup of wine and say:

GRACE AFTER THE MEAL

בָּרֵךְ

שִׁיר הַמַּעֲלוֹת: בְּשׁוּב יְיָ אֶת שִׁיבַת צִיּוֹן
הָיִינוּ כְּחֹלְמִים. אָז יִמָּלֵא שְׂחוֹק פִּינוּ וּלְשׁוֹנֵנוּ
רִנָּה. אָז יֹאמְרוּ בַגּוֹיִם: הִגְדִּיל יְיָ לַעֲשׂוֹת
עִם אֵלֶּה. הִגְדִּיל יְיָ לַעֲשׂוֹת עִמָּנוּ, הָיִינוּ
שְׂמֵחִים. שׁוּבָה יְיָ אֶת שְׁבִיתֵנוּ כַּאֲפִיקִים
בַּנֶּגֶב. הַזֹּרְעִים בְּדִמְעָה, בְּרִנָּה יִקְצֹרוּ. הָלוֹךְ
יֵלֵךְ וּבָכֹה נֹשֵׂא מֶשֶׁךְ הַזָּרַע, בֹּא יָבוֹא בְרִנָּה
נֹשֵׂא אֲלֻמֹּתָיו.

If it were up to me,
I'd give the Egyptians 4 plagues,
and the Jewish people
10 cups of wine!

A song of Ascents: When God brings back the exiles to Zion, we will have been like dreamers. Then our mouths will be filled with laughter, and our tongues with glad song. Then it will be said among the nations: God has done great things for us, and we were happy. Restore our captives like streams in the dry land. Those who plant in tears will harvest in joy. Though the farmer plants the field in tears, he will come home with joy with his sheaves.

רַבּוֹתַי נְבָרֵךְ.
יְהִי שֵׁם יְיָ מְבֹרָךְ מֵעַתָּה וְעַד עוֹלָם.
בִּרְשׁוּת מָרָנָן וְרַבּוֹתַי, נְבָרֵךְ (אֱלֹהֵינוּ) שֶׁאָכַלְנוּ מִשֶּׁלוֹ.
בָּרוּךְ (אֱלֹהֵינוּ) שֶׁאָכַלְנוּ מִשֶּׁלוֹ וּבְטוּבוֹ חָיִינוּ.
בָּרוּךְ (אֱלֹהֵינוּ) שֶׁאָכַלְנוּ מִשֶּׁלוֹ וּבְטוּבוֹ חָיִינוּ.
בָּרוּךְ הוּא וּבָרוּךְ שְׁמוֹ.

If three or more males, aged thirteen or older, ate together, the leader says: Gentlemen let us say Grace.

The group responds: Blessed in the Name of God from this moment and forever!

The leader continues: Blessed in the Name of God from this moment and forever!

With the permission of the distinguished people present let us bless (*If ten men:* our God) for we have eaten from what is His.

The group responds: Blessed is He (our God) of Whose we have eaten and through Whose goodness we live.

The leader continues: Blessed is He (our God) of Whose we have eaten and through Whose goodness we live.

If ten men: Blessed is He and blessed is His Name.

בָּרוּךְ אַתָּה יְיָ אֱלֹהֵינוּ מֶלֶךְ הָעוֹלָם הַזָּן אֶת הָעוֹלָם כֻּלּוֹ בְּטוּבוֹ בְּחֵן בְּחֶסֶד וּבְרַחֲמִים הוּא נוֹתֵן לֶחֶם לְכָל בָּשָׂר כִּי לְעוֹלָם חַסְדּוֹ. וּבְטוּבוֹ הַגָּדוֹל תָּמִיד לֹא חָסַר לָנוּ וְאַל יֶחְסַר לָנוּ מָזוֹן לְעוֹלָם וָעֶד. בַּעֲבוּר שְׁמוֹ הַגָּדוֹל— כִּי הוּא אֵל זָן וּמְפַרְנֵס לַכֹּל, וּמֵיטִיב לַכֹּל, וּמֵכִין מָזוֹן לְכָל בְּרִיּוֹתָיו אֲשֶׁר בָּרָא. בָּרוּךְ אַתָּה יְיָ הַזָּן אֶת-הַכֹּל.

Blessed are You, God, King of the universe, Who nourishes the entire world; in His goodness, with grace, with loving kindness, and with mercy. He gives nourishment to everything living, because His loving kindness is forever. And through His great goodness we never ran out of nourishment and may never run out of it in the future. Because His Great Name, because He is the God Who nourishes and makes everything live, and benefits all, and He prepares food for all of His creatures which He has created. Blessed are You, God, Who nourishes all.

נוֹדֶה לְךָ יְיָ אֱלֹהֵינוּ עַל שֶׁהִנְחַלְתָּ לַאֲבוֹתֵינוּ אֶרֶץ חֶמְדָּה טוֹבָה וּרְחָבָה, וְעַל שֶׁהוֹצֵאתָנוּ יְיָ אֱלֹהֵינוּ מֵאֶרֶץ מִצְרַיִם, וּפְדִיתָנוּ מִבֵּית עֲבָדִים, וְעַל בְּרִיתְךָ שֶׁחָתַמְתָּ בִּבְשָׂרֵנוּ, וְעַל תּוֹרָתְךָ שֶׁלִּמַּדְתָּנוּ, וְעַל חֻקֶּיךָ שֶׁהוֹדַעְתָּנוּ, וְעַל חַיִּים חֵן וָחֶסֶד שֶׁחוֹנַנְתָּנוּ, וְעַל אֲכִילַת מָזוֹן שָׁאַתָּה זָן וּמְפַרְנֵס אוֹתָנוּ תָּמִיד בְּכָל יוֹם וּבְכָל עֵת וּבְכָל שָׁעָה.

We thank You, God, because You have given to our ancestors a valuable, good and spacious land; because You rescued us, God, our God, from the land of Egypt and You freed us from slavery; because Your agreement which You sealed in our flesh; because Your Torah which You taught us and because Your laws which you made use aware; because life, grace, and loving kindness which You gave us; and because the food with which You nourish and support us constantly, in every day, in every season, and in every hour.

Bitsy is using a new toothbrush and special toothpaste for the holiday.

וְעַל הַכֹּל יְיָ אֱלֹהֵינוּ אֲנַחְנוּ מוֹדִים לָךְ וּמְבָרְכִים אוֹתָךְ. יִתְבָּרַךְ שִׁמְךָ בְּפִי כָּל חַי תָּמִיד לְעוֹלָם וָעֶד. כַּכָּתוּב: וְאָכַלְתָּ וְשָׂבָעְתָּ וּבֵרַכְתָּ אֶת יְיָ אֱלֹהֶיךָ עַל הָאָרֶץ הַטֹּבָה אֲשֶׁר נָתַן לָךְ. בָּרוּךְ אַתָּה יְיָ עַל הָאָרֶץ וְעַל הַמָּזוֹן.

Because of all this, God, we thank You and bless You. May Your Name be blessed forever by everything living. Because it is written: 'And you should eat and be satisfied and bless God for the good land which He gave you.' Blessed are You, God, for the land and for the food.

רַחֶם נָא יְיָ אֱלֹהֵינוּ עַל יִשְׂרָאֵל עַמֶּךָ, וְעַל יְרוּשָׁלַיִם עִירֶךָ, וְעַל צִיּוֹן מִשְׁכַּן כְּבוֹדֶךָ וְעַל מַלְכוּת בֵּית דָּוִד מְשִׁיחֶךָ, וְעַל הַבַּיִת הַגָּדוֹל וְהַקָּדוֹשׁ שֶׁנִּקְרָא שִׁמְךָ עָלָיו. אֱלֹהֵינוּ אָבִינוּ רְעֵנוּ זוּנֵנוּ פַּרְנְסֵנוּ וְכַלְכְּלֵנוּ וְהַרְוִיחֵנוּ וְהַרְוַח לָנוּ, יְיָ אֱלֹהֵינוּ מְהֵרָה מִכָּל צָרוֹתֵינוּ. וְנָא אַל תַּצְרִיכֵנוּ, יְיָ אֱלֹהֵינוּ, לֹא לִידֵי מַתְּנַת בָּשָׂר וָדָם וְלֹא לִידֵי הַלְוָאָתָם, כִּי אִם לְיָדְךָ הַמְּלֵאָה, הַפְּתוּחָה הַגְּדוּשָׁה וְהָרְחָבָה, שֶׁלֹּא נֵבוֹשׁ וְלֹא נִכָּלֵם לְעוֹלָם וָעֶד.

Have mercy God, on Your people Israel, on Your city Jerusalem, on Zion, the resting place of Your Glory, on the ruling house of David, Your chosen, and on the great and holy House on which Your Name is called. Our God, our Father — take care of us, nourish us, sustain us, support us, relieve us; God, our God, grant us fast relief from all our troubles. Please, God, our God, make us not needful of the gifts of human hands nor of their loans — but only of Your Hand that is full, open, holy, and generous, so that we will not feel inner shame or be humiliated for ever and ever.

On the Sabbath say the following paragraph.

רְצֵה וְהַחֲלִיצֵנוּ יְיָ אֱלֹהֵינוּ בְּמִצְוֹתֶיךָ וּבְמִצְוַת יוֹם הַשְּׁבִיעִי, הַשַּׁבָּת הַגָּדוֹל וְהַקָּדוֹשׁ הַזֶּה. כִּי יוֹם זֶה גָּדוֹל וְקָדוֹשׁ הוּא לְפָנֶיךָ לִשְׁבָּת בּוֹ וְלָנוּחַ בּוֹ בְּאַהֲבָה, כְּמִצְוַת רְצוֹנֶךָ. וּבִרְצוֹנְךָ הָנַח לָנוּ, יְיָ אֱלֹהֵינוּ, שֶׁלֹּא תְהֵא צָרָה וְיָגוֹן וַאֲנָחָה בְּיוֹם מְנוּחָתֵנוּ, וְהַרְאֵנוּ, יְיָ אֱלֹהֵינוּ, בְּנֶחָמַת צִיּוֹן עִירֶךָ וּבְבִנְיַן יְרוּשָׁלַיִם עִיר קָדְשֶׁךָ, כִּי אַתָּה הוּא בַּעַל הַיְשׁוּעוֹת וּבַעַל הַנֶּחָמוֹת.

May it please You, God — give us rest through Your commandments and through the commandment of the seventh day, this great and holy Sabbath. For this day is great and holy before You to rest on it and be content on it in love, as you ordered. May You want, GOD, our God, that there be no worry, grief, or mourning on this day of our contentment. And show us, God, our God, the comfort of Zion, Your city, and the rebuilding of Jerusalem, city of Your holiness, for You are the Master of salvations and Master of comforts.

אֱלֹהֵינוּ וֵאלֹהֵי אֲבוֹתֵינוּ, יַעֲלֶה וְיָבֹא וְיַגִּיעַ
וְיֵרָאֶה וְיֵרָצֶה וְיִשָּׁמַע וְיִפָּקֵד וְיִזָּכֵר זִכְרוֹנֵנוּ
וּפִקְדוֹנֵנוּ וְזִכְרוֹן אֲבוֹתֵינוּ, וְזִכְרוֹן מָשִׁיחַ בֶּן
דָּוִד עַבְדֶּךָ, וְזִכְרוֹן יְרוּשָׁלַיִם עִיר קָדְשֶׁךָ, וְזִכְרוֹן
כָּל עַמְּךָ בֵּית יִשְׂרָאֵל לְפָנֶיךָ, לִפְלֵיטָה לְטוֹבָה
לְחֵן וּלְחֶסֶד וּלְרַחֲמִים לְחַיִּים וּלְשָׁלוֹם בְּיוֹם
חַג הַמַּצּוֹת הַזֶּה. זָכְרֵנוּ יְיָ אֱלֹהֵינוּ בּוֹ לְטוֹבָה,
וּפָקְדֵנוּ בוֹ לִבְרָכָה, וְהוֹשִׁיעֵנוּ בוֹ לְחַיִּים טוֹבִים.
וּבִדְבַר יְשׁוּעָה וְרַחֲמִים חוּס וְחָנֵּנוּ וְרַחֵם עָלֵינוּ
וְהוֹשִׁיעֵנוּ, כִּי אֵלֶיךָ עֵינֵינוּ, כִּי אֵל מֶלֶךְ חַנּוּן
וְרַחוּם אָתָּה.

Our God and God of our fathers, may there rise, come, reach, be noted, be favored, be heard, be considered, and be remembered before You — the memory and consideration of ourselves, the memory of our fathers; the memory of Messiah, son of David, Your servant; the memory of Jerusalem, Your holy city; and the memory of Your entire people, the House of Israel — for deliverance, for well-being, for grace, for loving kindness, and for mercy, for life and for peace on this day of the Festival of Matzos. Remember us on it, God, our God, for goodness, consider us on it for blessing, and help us on it for (good) life. Concerning salvation and mercy, have pity, show grace and be merciful on us and help us. Because our eyes are turned to You; because You are the Almighty, gracious, and generous.

וּבְנֵה יְרוּשָׁלַיִם עִיר הַקֹּדֶשׁ בִּמְהֵרָה בְיָמֵינוּ.
בָּרוּךְ אַתָּה יְיָ, בּוֹנֵה בְרַחֲמָיו יְרוּשָׁלָיִם. אָמֵן.

Rebuild Jerusalem, the Holy City, soon in our days. Blessed are You, God, Who rebuilds Jerusalem (in His mercy). Amen.

OODYS GUIDE FOR THE PERPLEXED

(and the somewhat confused)

"See, Bitsy, the Israelites were waiting for the order from Moses to sneak out of Egypt during the night. Moses didn't want the Egyptians to know of their plan, so he *inscribed* all the unleavened bread with the time of departure in *secret Braille Code*. That way the Israelites could read it even during the *Plague of Darkness!* Here, can you feel the marks on this *matzah*?. The Israelites then quickly ate the matzah before the secret message got into the wrong hands! And *that's* why the matzah looks and feels the way it does today!"

"Wow!"

"Not!!"

בָּרוּךְ אַתָּה יְיָ, אֱלֹהֵינוּ מֶלֶךְ הָעוֹלָם, הָאֵל אָבִינוּ מַלְכֵּנוּ אַדִּירֵנוּ בּוֹרְאֵנוּ גּוֹאֲלֵנוּ יוֹצְרֵנוּ קְדוֹשֵׁנוּ קְדוֹשׁ יַעֲקֹב, רוֹעֵנוּ רוֹעֵה יִשְׂרָאֵל, הַמֶּלֶךְ הַטּוֹב וְהַמֵּטִיב לַכֹּל, שֶׁבְּכָל יוֹם וָיוֹם הוּא הֵיטִיב, הוּא מֵיטִיב, הוּא יֵיטִיב לָנוּ; הוּא גְמָלָנוּ, הוּא גוֹמְלֵנוּ, הוּא יִגְמְלֵנוּ לָעַד, לְחֵן וּלְחֶסֶד וּלְרַחֲמִים וּלְרֶוַח הַצָּלָה וְהַצְלָחָה בְּרָכָה וִישׁוּעָה נֶחָמָה פַּרְנָסָה וְכַלְכָּלָה וְרַחֲמִים וְחַיִּים וְשָׁלוֹם וְכָל טוֹב; וּמִכָּל טוּב לְעוֹלָם אַל יְחַסְּרֵנוּ.

Blessed are You, God, King of the universe, the Almighty, our Father, our King, our Ruler, our Creator, our Redeemer, our Maker, our Holy One, Holy One of Jacob,Shepherd, the Shepherd of Israel, the good and generous King. Because every single day He did good, does good, and will do good to us. He was generous with us, is generous with us, and will forever be generous with us — with grace and with loving kindness and with mercy, with relief, salvation, success, blessing, help, comfort, livelihood, support, mercy, life, peace, and all good; and of all good things may He never hold back from us..

הָרַחֲמָן הוּא יִמְלוֹךְ עָלֵינוּ לְעוֹלָם וָעֶד הָרַחֲמָן הוּא יִתְבָּרַךְ בַּשָּׁמַיִם וּבָאָרֶץ. הָרַחֲמָן הוּא יִשְׁתַּבַּח לְדוֹר דּוֹרִים, וְיִתְפָּאַר בָּנוּ לָעַד וּלְנֵצַח נְצָחִים וְיִתְהַדַּר בָּנוּ לָעַד וּלְעוֹלְמֵי עוֹלָמִים. הָרַחֲמָן הוּא יְפַרְנְסֵנוּ בְּכָבוֹד. הָרַחֲמָן הוּא יִשְׁבּוֹר עֻלֵּנוּ מֵעַל צַוָּארֵנוּ, וְהוּא יוֹלִיכֵנוּ קוֹמְמִיּוּת לְאַרְצֵנוּ. הָרַחֲמָן הוּא יִשְׁלַח לָנוּ, בְּרָכָה מְרֻבָּה בַּבַּיִת הַזֶּה, וְעַל שֻׁלְחָן זֶה שֶׁאָכַלְנוּ עָלָיו. הָרַחֲמָן הוּא יִשְׁלַח לָנוּ אֶת אֵלִיָּהוּ הַנָּבִיא זָכוּר לַטּוֹב, וִיבַשֶּׂר לָנוּ בְּשׂוֹרוֹת טוֹבוֹת יְשׁוּעוֹת וְנֶחָמוֹת. הָרַחֲמָן הוּא יְבָרֵךְ אֶת אָבִי מוֹרִי בַּעַל הַבַּיִת הַזֶּה, וְאֶת אִמִּי מוֹרָתִי, בַּעֲלַת הַבַּיִת הַזֶּה, אוֹתָם וְאֶת בֵּיתָם, וְאֶת זַרְעָם וְאֶת כָּל אֲשֶׁר לָהֶם.

The compassionate One! May He rule us forever. The compassionate One! May He be blessed on heaven and on earth. The compassionate One! May He be praised throughout all generations, may He be glorified through us until the end, and be honored through us to the unexplainable everlasting. The compassionate One! May He support us in honor. The compassionate One! May He break the shackles of hardship from our necks and guide us upright to our Land. The compassionate One! May He send us many blessings to this house and upon this table at which we have eaten. The compassionate One! May He send us Elijah, the Prophet — may he be remembered for good — to bring us good news, salvations, and comfort. The compassionate One! May He bless

Children at their parents' table add the words:

(my father, my teacher) the master of this house, and (my mother, my teacher) lady of this house, together with their household, their children and everything that is theirs.

Those eating at their own table say: me (my wife/husband and family) and all that is mine, *All guests say:* them, their house, their family, and all that is theirs,
All continue here: ours and all that is ours — just as our ancestors Abraham, Isaac, and Jacob were blessed in everything, from everything, with everything. So may He bless us all together with a perfect blessing. And let us say: Amen!

On high, may merit be pleaded on them and on us, to keep peace. May we receive a blessing from God and kindness from the God of our salvation, and find favor and understanding in the eyes of God and man.
On the Sabbath add: The compassionate One! May He let us arrive at the day which will be completely a Sabbath and rest day for eternal life.
The compassionate One! May He cause us to arrive at that day which is good, (that everlasting day, the day when the just will sit with crowns on their heads, enjoying the reflection of God's Majesty — and may our portion be with them!).
The compassionate One! May He make us worthy to live in the days of Messiah and in the life of the World to Come. He Who is a tower of salvations to His king and shows loving kindness to His chosen, to David and his descendants forever. He Who makes harmony in His heavenly heights, may He make harmony for us and for all Israel. Say: Amen!
Fear God, His holy ones, for those who fear Him feel no loss. Young lions may feel need and hunger, but those who look for God will not lack any good. Give thanks to God for He is good; His loving kindness is forever. You open Your hand and satisfy the desire of every living thing. Blessed is the

אוֹתִי וְאֶת אִשְׁתִּי וְאֶת זַרְעִי, אוֹתָנוּ וְאֶת כָּל אֲשֶׁר לָנוּ, כְּמוֹ שֶׁנִּתְבָּרְכוּ אֲבוֹתֵינוּ אַבְרָהָם יִצְחָק וְיַעֲקֹב בַּכֹּל מִכֹּל כֹּל, כֵּן יְבָרֵךְ אוֹתָנוּ, כֻּלָּנוּ יַחַד, בִּבְרָכָה שְׁלֵמָה, וְנֹאמַר: אָמֵן.

בַּמָּרוֹם יְלַמְּדוּ (עָלָיו וְ) עָלֵינוּ זְכוּת, שֶׁתְּהֵא לְמִשְׁמֶרֶת שָׁלוֹם, וְנִשָּׂא בְרָכָה מֵאֵת יְיָ, וּצְדָקָה מֵאֱלֹהֵי יִשְׁעֵנוּ, וְנִמְצָא חֵן וְשֵׂכֶל טוֹב בְּעֵינֵי אֱלֹהִים וְאָדָם.

On the Sabbath add:

הָרַחֲמָן הוּא יַנְחִילֵנוּ לְיוֹם שֶׁכֻּלּוֹ שַׁבָּת וּמְנוּחָה, לְחַיֵּי הָעוֹלָמִים.
הָרַחֲמָן הוּא יַנְחִילֵנוּ לְיוֹם שֶׁכֻּלּוֹ טוֹב.

הָרַחֲמָן הוּא יְזַכֵּנוּ לִימוֹת הַמָּשִׁיחַ וּלְחַיֵּי הָעוֹלָם הַבָּא.

מִגְדּוֹל יְשׁוּעוֹת מַלְכּוֹ, וְעֹשֶׂה חֶסֶד לִמְשִׁיחוֹ, לְדָוִד וּלְזַרְעוֹ עַד עוֹלָם. עֹשֶׂה שָׁלוֹם בִּמְרוֹמָיו הוּא יַעֲשֶׂה שָׁלוֹם עָלֵינוּ וְעַל כָּל יִשְׂרָאֵל, וְאִמְרוּ: אָמֵן.

יְראוּ אֶת יְיָ קְדֹשָׁיו, כִּי אֵין מַחְסוֹר לִירֵאָיו. כְּפִירִים רָשׁוּ וְרָעֵבוּ וְדֹרְשֵׁי יְיָ לֹא יַחְסְרוּ כָל טוֹב. הוֹדוּ לַיְיָ כִּי טוֹב כִּי לְעוֹלָם חַסְדּוֹ. פּוֹתֵחַ אֶת יָדֶךָ, וּמַשְׂבִּיעַ לְכָל חַי רָצוֹן.

בָּרוּךְ הַגֶּבֶר אֲשֶׁר יִבְטַח בַּיְיָ, וְהָיָה יְיָ מִבְטַחוֹ. נַעַר הָיִיתִי, גַּם זָקַנְתִּי, וְלֹא רָאִיתִי צַדִּיק נֶעֱזָב, וְזַרְעוֹ מְבַקֶּשׁ לָחֶם. יְיָ עֹז לְעַמּוֹ יִתֵּן, יְיָ יְבָרֵךְ אֶת עַמּוֹ בַשָּׁלוֹם.

man who trusts in God, and God will be his trust. I was a youth and also have aged, and I have not seen a good man ignored, with his children begging for bread. God will give might to His nation; God will bless His nation with peace.

Zady, why do you keep your talit and tefillin at your bedside?
The Shofar of the Messiah may wake us in the middle of the night. How can we leave without these things which are so dear to us?

Say the blessing over wine and drink the third cup.

בָּרוּךְ אַתָּה יְיָ, אֱלֹהֵינוּ מֶלֶךְ הָעוֹלָם, בּוֹרֵא פְּרִי הַגָּפֶן.

Blessed are You, God, King of the universe, Who creates the fruit of the vine.

Pour the fourth cup, open the door and say:

שְׁפֹךְ חֲמָתְךָ אֶל הַגּוֹיִם אֲשֶׁר לֹא יְדָעוּךָ, וְעַל מַמְלָכוֹת אֲשֶׁר בְּשִׁמְךָ לֹא
קָרָאוּ. כִּי אָכַל אֶת יַעֲקֹב. וְאֶת נָוֵהוּ הֵשַׁמּוּ. שְׁפָךְ עֲלֵיהֶם זַעְמֶךָ, וַחֲרוֹן
אַפְּךָ יַשִּׂיגֵם. תִּרְדֹּף בְּאַף וְתַשְׁמִידֵם, מִתַּחַת שְׁמֵי יְיָ.

Pour Your wrath on the nations that do not accept You and on the kingdoms that do not say Your Name. Because they have overcome Jacob and destroyed the place where He lives. Pour Your anger on them and let Your fiery anger overtake them. Chase them with anger and destroy them from under the heavens of God.

Close the door and continue.

During the days of the second Temple, Rabbi Huna would open his door and call out, "Whoever is hungry let them come and eat"
Where's the dog off to in such a hurry?
!!
?
!
!
?

הַלֵּל

PSALMS OF PRAISE

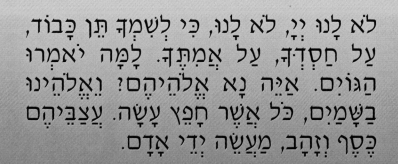

לֹא לָנוּ יְיָ, לֹא לָנוּ, כִּי לְשִׁמְךָ תֵּן כָּבוֹד,
עַל חַסְדְּךָ, עַל אֲמִתֶּךָ. לָמָּה יֹאמְרוּ
הַגּוֹיִם. אַיֵּה נָא אֱלֹהֵיהֶם? וֵאלֹהֵינוּ
בַשָּׁמָיִם, כֹּל אֲשֶׁר חָפֵץ עָשָׂה. עֲצַבֵּיהֶם
כֶּסֶף וְזָהָב, מַעֲשֵׂה יְדֵי אָדָם.

פֶּה לָהֶם וְלֹא יְדַבֵּרוּ, עֵינַיִם לָהֶם וְלֹא יִרְאוּ. אָזְנַיִם לָהֶם וְלֹא יִשְׁמָעוּ, אַף לָהֶם
וְלֹא יְרִיחוּן. יְדֵיהֶם — וְלֹא יְמִישׁוּן, רַגְלֵיהֶם — וְלֹא יְהַלֵּכוּ, לֹא יֶהְגּוּ בִּגְרוֹנָם.
כְּמוֹהֶם יִהְיוּ עֹשֵׂיהֶם, כֹּל אֲשֶׁר בֹּטֵחַ בָּהֶם. יִשְׂרָאֵל בְּטַח בַּיָי — עֶזְרָם וּמָגִנָּם
הוּא. בֵּית אַהֲרֹן בִּטְחוּ בַיָי — עֶזְרָם וּמָגִנָּם הוּא. יִרְאֵי יְיָ בִּטְחוּ בַיָי — עֶזְרָם
וּמָגִנָּם הוּא.

Not for us, O Lord, not for us, but for You give glory, because of Your kindness and Your truth! Why should the nations say: 'Where is their God?' Our God is in the heavens; whatever He pleases, He does! Their idols are silver and gold, made by man. They have a mouth, but cannot speak; they have eyes, but cannot see; they have ears, but cannot hear; they have a nose, but cannot smell; their hands — they cannot feel; their feet — they cannot walk; nor can they utter a sound with their throat. Those who make them should become like them, whoever believes in them! O Israel! Believe in God — He is their help and protector! House of Aaron! Believe in God! He is their help and protector. You who fear God! — trust in God, He is their help and protector!

A fragment of the mosaic floor of a synagogue in Northern Israel, dated 1600 years ago. In it, Spring is represented as a maiden holding a basket containing the fruits of the season.

יְיָ זְכָרָנוּ יְבָרֵךְ; יְבָרֵךְ אֶת בֵּית יִשְׂרָאֵל, יְבָרֵךְ אֶת בֵּית אַהֲרֹן, יְבָרֵךְ יִרְאֵי יְיָ, הַקְּטַנִּים עִם הַגְּדֹלִים. יֹסֵף יְיָ עֲלֵיכֶם, עֲלֵיכֶם וְעַל בְּנֵיכֶם. בְּרוּכִים אַתֶּם לַייָ, עֹשֵׂה שָׁמַיִם וָאָרֶץ. הַשָּׁמַיִם שָׁמַיִם לַייָ. וְהָאָרֶץ נָתַן לִבְנֵי אָדָם. לֹא הַמֵּתִים יְהַלְלוּיָהּ. וְלֹא כָּל יֹרְדֵי דוּמָה. וַאֲנַחְנוּ נְבָרֵךְ יָהּ מֵעַתָּה וְעַד עוֹלָם הַלְלוּיָהּ.

God Who has remembered us will bless — He will bless the House of Aaron; He will bless those who respect God, the small as well as the great. May God make your family grow, and the family of your children! You are blessed of God, maker of heaven and earth. As for the heaven — the heaven is God's, but the earth, He has given to mankind. The dead can't praise God or those who are silent; but we will bless God now and forever. Halleluyah!

אָהַבְתִּי כִּי יִשְׁמַע יְיָ. אֶת קוֹלִי, תַּחֲנוּנָי; כִּי הִטָּה אָזְנוֹ לִי. וּבְיָמַי אֶקְרָא: אֲפָפוּנִי חֶבְלֵי מָוֶת, וּמְצָרֵי שְׁאוֹל מְצָאוּנִי, צָרָה וְיָגוֹן אֶמְצָא. וּבְשֵׁם יְיָ אֶקְרָא: אָנָּה יְיָ, מַלְּטָה נַפְשִׁי! חַנּוּן יְיָ וְצַדִּיק, וֵאלֹהֵינוּ מְרַחֵם. שֹׁמֵר פְּתָאִים יְיָ, דַּלֹּתִי וְלִי יְהוֹשִׁיעַ. שׁוּבִי נַפְשִׁי לִמְנוּחָיְכִי, כִּי יְיָ גָּמַל עָלָיְכִי. כִּי חִלַּצְתָּ נַפְשִׁי מִמָּוֶת, אֶת עֵינִי מִן דִּמְעָה, אֶת רַגְלִי מִדֶּחִי. אֶתְהַלֵּךְ לִפְנֵי יְיָ. בְּאַרְצוֹת הַחַיִּים. הֶאֱמַנְתִּי כִּי אֲדַבֵּר, אֲנִי עָנִיתִי מְאֹד. אֲנִי אָמַרְתִּי בְחָפְזִי: כָּל הָאָדָם כֹּזֵב.

I love Him for God hears my voice, my request. For He has listened to me, I will turn to Him forever. The ropes of death surround me; the boundaries of the grave have found me; I have found trouble and sorrow. Then I called on God: 'Please God, save my soul', Gracious is God and good, our God is compassionate. The Lord protects the simple; I was at my worst but He saved me. Return to your rest, my soul, for God has been kind to you. You saved my soul from death, my eyes from tears and my feet from stumbling. I will walk before the Lord in the lands of the living. I believe although I say: 'I suffer greatly.' I said in my haste: 'All mankind is dishonest.'

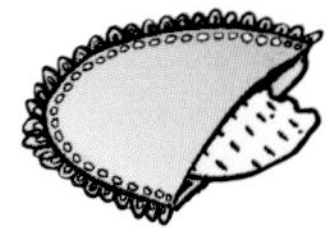

מָה אָשִׁיב לַייָ, כָּל תַּגְמוּלוֹהִי עָלָי? כּוֹס יְשׁוּעוֹת אֶשָּׂא. וּבְשֵׁם יְיָ אֶקְרָא. נְדָרַי לַייָ אֲשַׁלֵּם. נֶגְדָה נָּא לְכָל עַמּוֹ. יָקָר בְּעֵינֵי יְיָ. הַמָּוְתָה לַחֲסִידָיו. אָנָּה יְיָ, כִּי אֲנִי עַבְדֶּךָ, אֲנִי עַבְדְּךָ בֶּן אֲמָתֶךָ, פִּתַּחְתָּ לְמוֹסֵרָי.

How can I repay God for all His kindness to me? I will raise the cup of freedom, and say the Name of God. I will promise to God in the presence of His entire people. The death of His devout ones is precious in the eyes of God. Please, God — because I am Your servant, I am Your servant, one of Your maids — You have freed

לְךָ אֶזְבַּח זֶבַח תּוֹדָה, וּבְשֵׁם יְיָ אֶקְרָא. נְדָרַי לַיָי אֲשַׁלֵּם נֶגְדָה נָּא לְכָל עַמּוֹ. בְּחַצְרוֹת בֵּית יְיָ, בְּתוֹכֵכִי יְרוּשָׁלָיִם. הַלְלוּיָהּ!

me. I sacrifice thanksgiving offerings to You, and I will say the Name of God. I will pay my vows to God in front of His entire people; in the courtyards of the House of God, in front of you, Jerusalem. Halleluyah!

הַלְלוּ אֶת יְיָ כָּל גּוֹיִם, שַׁבְּחוּהוּ כָּל הָאֻמִּים. כִּי גָבַר עָלֵינוּ חַסְדּוֹ, וֶאֱמֶת יְיָ לְעוֹלָם. הַלְלוּיָהּ!

Praise God, all you nations; praise Him, all you peoples! For His kindness to us was great, and the truth of God is everlasting. Halleluyah!

הוֹדוּ לַיָי. כִּי טוֹב, כִּי לְעוֹלָם חַסְדּוֹ!

Give thanks to God for He is good; His kindness lasts forever!

יֹאמַר נָא יִשְׂרָאֵל, כִּי לְעוֹלָם חַסְדּוֹ!

Let Israel say: His kindness lasts forever!

יֹאמְרוּ נָא בֵית אַהֲרֹן, כִּי לְעוֹלָם חַסְדּוֹ!

Let the House of Aaron say: His kindness lasts forever!

יֹאמְרוּ נָא יִרְאֵי יְיָ, כִּי לְעוֹלָם חַסְדּוֹ!

Let those who respect God say: His kindness lasts forever!

מִן הַמֵּצַר קָרָאתִי יָּהּ, עָנָנִי בַמֶּרְחַבְיָה. יְיָ לִי לֹא אִירָא. מַה יַּעֲשֶׂה לִי אָדָם? יְיָ לִי בְּעֹזְרָי, וַאֲנִי אֶרְאֶה בְשֹׂנְאָי. טוֹב לַחֲסוֹת בַּיָי. מִבְּטֹחַ בָּאָדָם. טוֹב לַחֲסוֹת בַּיָי. מִבְּטֹחַ בִּנְדִיבִים. כָּל גּוֹיִם סְבָבוּנִי, בְּשֵׁם יְיָ כִּי אֲמִילַם. סַבּוּנִי גַם סְבָבוּנִי, בְּשֵׁם יְיָ כִּי אֲמִילַם. סַבּוּנִי כִדְבוֹרִים, דֹּעֲכוּ כְּאֵשׁ קוֹצִים, בְּשֵׁם יְיָ כִּי אֲמִילַם. דָּחֹה דְחִיתַנִי לִנְפֹּל, וַיָי עֲזָרָנִי. עָזִּי וְזִמְרָת יָהּ, וַיְהִי לִי לִישׁוּעָה. קוֹל רִנָּה וִישׁוּעָה בְּאָהֳלֵי צַדִּיקִים: יְמִין יְיָ עֹשָׂה חָיִל, יְמִין יְיָ רוֹמֵמָה, יְמִין יְיָ עֹשָׂה חָיִל.

Out of distress I called to God; God answered me with wisdom. God is with me, I have no fear; how can man worry me? God is here for me through my helpers; so I can face my enemies. It is better to let God protect me than to trust man. It is better to let God protect me than to trust in princes. All nations surround me; but in the Name of God I cut them down. They surround me. They swarm around me; but in the Name of God, I cut them down! They swarm around me like bees, but they are put out as thorns put out a fire; in the Name of God I cut them down! You pushed me hard so that I should fall, but God helped me. God is my strength and song; He became the one to save me. The sound of happiness and salvation is in the tents of the good: 'The right hand of God does

לֹא אָמוּת, כִּי אֶחְיֶה, וַאֲסַפֵּר מַעֲשֵׂי יָהּ. יַסֹּר יִסְּרַנִּי יָּהּ. וְלַמָּוֶת לֹא נְתָנָנִי. פִּתְחוּ לִי שַׁעֲרֵי צֶדֶק, אָבֹא בָם, אוֹדֶה יָהּ. זֶה הַשַּׁעַר לַיְיָ, צַדִּיקִים יָבֹאוּ בוֹ.

אוֹדְךָ, כִּי עֲנִיתָנִי, וַתְּהִי לִי לִישׁוּעָה. אֶבֶן מָאֲסוּ הַבּוֹנִים, הָיְתָה לְרֹאשׁ פִּנָּה. מֵאֵת יְיָ הָיְתָה זֹּאת הִיא נִפְלָאת בְּעֵינֵינוּ. זֶה הַיּוֹם עָשָׂה יְיָ, נָגִילָה וְנִשְׂמְחָה בוֹ!

well! The right hand of God is raised in success! The right hand of God does bravely!' I won't die! I will live and tell the deeds of God. God punished me greatly but He did not let me die. Open the gates of good for me, I will enter them and thank God. This is the gate of God; the good will enter through it. I thank You because You answered me and became the one to save me! The stone which the builders hated has become the cornerstone! The stone which the builders hated has become the cornerstone! This is because of God; it is wondrous in our eyes! This is because God; it is wondrous in our eyes! This is the day God has made; we will be happy and glad in Him! This is the day God has made; we will be happy and glad in Him!

אָנָּא יְיָ, הוֹשִׁיעָה נָּא!
אָנָּא יְיָ, הוֹשִׁיעָה נָּא!
אָנָּא יְיָ, הַצְלִיחָה נָּא!
אָנָּא יְיָ, הַצְלִיחָה נָּא!

O God, please save us!
O God, please save us!
O God, please make us successful!
O God, please make us successful!

בָּרוּךְ הַבָּא בְּשֵׁם יְיָ; בֵּרַכְנוּכֶם מִבֵּית יְיָ. אֵל יְיָ, וַיָּאֶר לָנוּ. אִסְרוּ חַג בַּעֲבֹתִים. עַד קַרְנוֹת הַמִּזְבֵּחַ. אֵלִי אַתָּה וְאוֹדֶךָּ, אֱלֹהַי — אֲרוֹמְמֶךָּ. הוֹדוּ לַיְיָ, כִּי טוֹב, כִּי לְעוֹלָם חַסְדּוֹ!

Blessed is the one who comes in the Name of God; we bless you from the House of God. Blessed be he who comes in the Name of God; we bless you from the House of God. God is God and He made it clear, tie the festival offering with rope to the corners of the altar. God is God and He made it clear, tie the festival offering with rope to the corners of the altar. You are my God and I will thank You; my God and I will support You. You are my God and I will thank You. Give thanks to God, for He is good; His kindness lives forever!

Rabbi Shalom of Belz said, "There are 3 exiles:
The *exile* of the Jews among the other nations;
The *exile* of the Jews among the other Jews; and
The *exile* of a man to himself, which is the hardest of all."
I thought this egg was the hardest of all!
Oh...
Now I get this exile business!

יְהַלְלוּךָ יְיָ אֱלֹהֵינוּ (עַל) כָּל מַעֲשֶׂיךָ, וַחֲסִידֶיךָ צַדִּיקִים עוֹשֵׂי רְצוֹנֶךָ; וְכָל עַמְּךָ בֵּית יִשְׂרָאֵל בְּרִנָּה יוֹדוּ וִיבָרְכוּ וִישַׁבְּחוּ וִיפָאֲרוּ וִירוֹמְמוּ וְיַעֲרִיצוּ וְיַקְדִּישׁוּ וְיַמְלִיכוּ אֶת שִׁמְךָ מַלְכֵּנוּ, כִּי לְךָ טוֹב לְהוֹדוֹת, וּלְשִׁמְךָ נָאֶה לְזַמֵּר, כִּי מֵעוֹלָם וְעַד עוֹלָם אַתָּה אֵל.

They will praise You, God our God for all Your works, along with Your holy followers, the good, who do what You ask, and Your entire people, the House of Israel, with joy will thank, bless, praise, glorify, support, honor, make holy, and remember Your name, our King! For it is fitting to give thanks to You, and it is proper to sing praises to Your name, because You are God forever.

Give thanks to God, for He is good; His kindness lives forever! Give thanks to the God of Gods; His kindness lives forever! Give thanks to the Master of masters; His kindness lives forever! To the only one Who does great wonders; His kindness lives forever! To the one Who made the heaven with understanding; His kindness lives forever! To the one Who stretched out the earth over the waters; His kindness lives forever! To the one Who made great scholars; His kindness lives forever! The sun to create the day; His kindness lives forever! The moon and the stars to create the night; His kindness lives forever! To the one Who attacked the Egyptians by slaying their firstborn; His kindness lives forever! And took Israel from that place; His kindness endures forever! With a strong hand and an outstretched arm; His kindness lives forever! Who divided the Sea of Reeds into two parts; His kindness lives forever! And made Israel pass through it; His kindness lives forever! And threw Pharaoh and his army into the Sea of Reeds; His kindness lives forever! To the one Who led His people through the wilderness; His kindness lives forever! To the one Who killed great kings; His kindness lives forever! And killed mighty kings; His kindness lives forever! Sichon, king of the Emorites; His kindness lives forever! And Og, king of Bashan; His kindness lives forever! And gave their land as a gift; His kindness lives forever! A gift to Israel His servant; His kindness lives forever! Who remembered us in our worst time; His kindness lives forever! And let us escape from our enemies; His kindness lives forever! He gives food to all living things; His kindness lives forever! Give thanks to God of heaven; His kindness lives forever!

הודו לַיי כִּי טוב כִּי לְעוֹלָם חַסְדּוֹ.

הודו לֵאלֹהֵי הָאֱלֹהִים כִּי לְעוֹלָם חַסְדּוֹ.

הודו לַאֲדֹנֵי הָאֲדֹנִים כִּי לְעוֹלָם חַסְדּוֹ.

לְעֹשֵׂה נִפְלָאוֹת גְּדֹלוֹת לְבַדּוֹ כִּי לְעוֹלָם חַסְדּוֹ.

לְעֹשֵׂה הַשָּׁמַיִם בִּתְבוּנָה כִּי לְעוֹלָם חַסְדּוֹ.

לְרוֹקַע הָאָרֶץ עַל הַמָּיִם כִּי לְעוֹלָם חַסְדּוֹ.

לְעֹשֵׂה אוֹרִים גְּדֹלִים כִּי לְעוֹלָם חַסְדּוֹ.

אֶת הַשֶּׁמֶשׁ לְמֶמְשֶׁלֶת בַּיּוֹם כִּי לְעוֹלָם חַסְדּוֹ.

אֶת הַיָּרֵחַ וְכוֹכָבִים לְמֶמְשְׁלוֹת בַּלָּיְלָה כל״ח.

לְמַכֵּה מִצְרַיִם בִּבְכוֹרֵיהֶם כִּי לְעוֹלָם חַסְדּוֹ.

וַיּוֹצֵא יִשְׂרָאֵל מִתּוֹכָם כִּי לְעוֹלָם חַסְדּוֹ.

בְּיָד חֲזָקָה וּבִזְרוֹעַ נְטוּיָה כִּי לְעוֹלָם חַסְדּוֹ.

לְגֹזֵר יַם סוּף לִגְזָרִים כִּי לְעוֹלָם חַסְדּוֹ.

וְהֶעֱבִיר יִשְׂרָאֵל בְּתוֹכוֹ כִּי לְעוֹלָם חַסְדּוֹ.

וְנִעֵר פַּרְעֹה וְחֵילוֹ בְיַם סוּף כִּי לְעוֹלָם חַסְדּוֹ.

לְמוֹלִיךְ עַמּוֹ בַּמִּדְבָּר כִּי לְעוֹלָם חַסְדּוֹ.

לְמַכֵּה מְלָכִים גְּדֹלִים כִּי לְעוֹלָם חַסְדּוֹ.

וַיַּהֲרֹג מְלָכִים אַדִּירִים כִּי לְעוֹלָם חַסְדּוֹ.

לְסִיחוֹן מֶלֶךְ הָאֱמֹרִי כִּי לְעוֹלָם חַסְדּוֹ.

וּלְעוֹג מֶלֶךְ הַבָּשָׁן כִּי לְעוֹלָם חַסְדּוֹ.

וְנָתַן אַרְצָם לְנַחֲלָה כִּי לְעוֹלָם חַסְדּוֹ.

נַחֲלָה לְיִשְׂרָאֵל עַבְדּוֹ כִּי לְעוֹלָם חַסְדּוֹ.

שֶׁבְּשִׁפְלֵנוּ זָכַר לָנוּ כִּי לְעוֹלָם חַסְדּוֹ.

וַיִּפְרְקֵנוּ מִצָּרֵינוּ כִּי לְעוֹלָם חַסְדּוֹ.

נֹתֵן לֶחֶם לְכָל בָּשָׂר כִּי לְעוֹלָם חַסְדּוֹ.

הודו לְאֵל הַשָּׁמָיִם כִּי לְעוֹלָם חַסְדּוֹ.

The soul of every living being will bless Your Name, God our God; the spirit of all living things will always glorify and honor You, our King. Forever, You are God, and except for You we have no King, redeemer or helper. O Rescuer, and Redeemer, Sustainer and Merciful One in every time of trouble and distress. We have no King but You — God of the first and of the last, God of all creatures, Master of all generations, Who is praised in many ways, Who guides His world with kindness and His creatures with mercy. God neither slumbers nor sleeps; He wakes up the sleepers and awakens the slumberers; He makes the mute speak and frees those who are tied; He supports the falling and raises up those who are bowed down. To You alone we give thanks.

נִשְׁמַת כָּל חַי תְּבָרֵךְ אֶת שִׁמְךָ
יְיָ אֱלֹהֵינוּ, וְרוּחַ כָּל בָּשָׂר תְּפָאֵר
וּתְרוֹמֵם זִכְרְךָ מַלְכֵּנוּ תָּמִיד. מִן
הָעוֹלָם וְעַד הָעוֹלָם אַתָּה אֵל,
וּמִבַּלְעָדֶיךָ אֵין לָנוּ מֶלֶךְ גּוֹאֵל
וּמוֹשִׁיעַ, פּוֹדֶה וּמַצִּיל, וּמְפַרְנֵס
וּמְרַחֵם בְּכָל עֵת צָרָה וְצוּקָה. אֵין
לָנוּ מֶלֶךְ אֶלָּא אָתָּה. אֱלֹהֵי
הָרִאשׁוֹנִים וְהָאַחֲרוֹנִים, אֱלוֹהַּ כָּל
בְּרִיּוֹת, אֲדוֹן כָּל תּוֹלָדוֹת, הַמְּהֻלָּל
בְּרֹב הַתִּשְׁבָּחוֹת, הַמְנַהֵג עוֹלָמוֹ
בְּחֶסֶד וּבְרִיּוֹתָיו בְּרַחֲמִים. וַיְיָ לֹא
יָנוּם וְלֹא יִישָׁן, הַמְעוֹרֵר יְשֵׁנִים,
וְהַמֵּקִיץ נִרְדָּמִים, וְהַמֵּשִׂיחַ אִלְּמִים,
וְהַמַּתִּיר אֲסוּרִים, וְהַסּוֹמֵךְ נוֹפְלִים,
וְהַזּוֹקֵף כְּפוּפִים. לְךָ לְבַדְּךָ אֲנַחְנוּ
מוֹדִים.

אִלּוּ פִינוּ מָלֵא שִׁירָה כַּיָּם, וּלְשׁוֹנֵנוּ רִנָּה כַּהֲמוֹן גַּלָּיו, וְשִׂפְתוֹתֵינוּ שֶׁבַח כְּמֶרְחֲבֵי רָקִיעַ, וְעֵינֵינוּ מְאִירוֹת כַּשֶּׁמֶשׁ וְכַיָּרֵחַ, וְיָדֵינוּ פְרוּשׂוֹת כְּנִשְׁרֵי שָׁמָיִם, וְרַגְלֵינוּ קַלּוֹת כָּאַיָּלוֹת - אֵין אֲנַחְנוּ מַסְפִּיקִים לְהוֹדוֹת לְךָ, יְיָ אֱלֹהֵינוּ וֵאלֹהֵי אֲבוֹתֵינוּ, וּלְבָרֵךְ אֶת שְׁמֶךָ, עַל אַחַת מֵאָלֶף, אֶלֶף אַלְפֵי אֲלָפִים וְרִבֵּי רְבָבוֹת פְּעָמִים הַטּוֹבוֹת שֶׁעָשִׂיתָ עִם אֲבוֹתֵינוּ וְעִמָּנוּ.

If our mouths were as full of song as the sea, and our tongues as full of joy as its many waves, and our lips as full of praise as the size of the heavens, and our eyes as brilliant as the sun and the moon, and our hands as outspread in prayer as the eagles of the sky and our feet as fast as deer — we still could not thank You enough, God and God of our fathers, and bless Your Name, for even one of the thousands upon thousands and countless upon countless favors, miracles and wonders, which You performed for our ancestors and for us.

מִמִּצְרַיִם גְּאַלְתָּנוּ יְיָ אֱלֹהֵינוּ, וּמִבֵּית עֲבָדִים פְּדִיתָנוּ בְּרָעָב זַנְתָּנוּ, וּבְשָׂבָע כִּלְכַּלְתָּנוּ, מֵחֶרֶב הִצַּלְתָּנוּ, וּמִדֶּבֶר מִלַּטְתָּנוּ, וּמֵחֳלָיִם רָעִים וְנֶאֱמָנִים דִּלִּיתָנוּ. עַד הֵנָּה עֲזָרוּנוּ רַחֲמֶיךָ, וְלֹא עֲזָבוּנוּ חֲסָדֶיךָ.

You freed us from Egypt, God, and rescued us from slavery. In famine You gave us food and in plenty You supported us. You saved us from the sword; from the plague You let us escape; and You protected us from harsh and endless diseases. Your mercy has helped us until now, and Your kindness has not turned away from us.

וְאַל תִּטְּשֵׁנוּ יְיָ אֱלֹהֵינוּ לָנֶצַח. עַל כֵּן אֵבָרִים שֶׁפִּלַּגְתָּ בָּנוּ, וְרוּחַ וּנְשָׁמָה שֶׁנָּפַחְתָּ בְּאַפֵּינוּ וְלָשׁוֹן אֲשֶׁר שַׂמְתָּ בְּפִינוּ הֵן הֵם יוֹדוּ וִיבָרְכוּ וִישַׁבְּחוּ וִיפָאֲרוּ, וִירוֹמְמוּ וְיַעֲרִיצוּ, וְיַקְדִּישׁוּ וְיַמְלִיכוּ אֶת שִׁמְךָ מַלְכֵּנוּ. כִּי כָל פֶּה לְךָ יוֹדֶה, וְכָל לָשׁוֹן לְךָ תִשָּׁבַע, וְכָל בֶּרֶךְ לְךָ תִכְרַע, וְכָל קוֹמָה לְפָנֶיךָ תִשְׁתַּחֲוֶה, וְכָל לְבָבוֹת יִירָאוּךָ, וְכָל קֶרֶב וּכְלָיוֹת יְזַמְּרוּ לִשְׁמֶךָ, כַּדָּבָר שֶׁכָּתוּב:

Do not ever leave us, God. So, the arms and legs which You gave us, and the spirit and soul which You breathed into our nostrils, and the tongue which You put in our mouth — they will all thank and bless, praise and glorify, raise, be devoted to, honor and pay respect to Your Name, our King forever. Because every mouth will thank You; every knee will bend to You; all who stand tall will bow down to You; all hearts will respect You; and men's innermost feelings and thoughts will sing praises to Your name, just as it is written:

כָּל עַצְמֹתַי תֹּאמַרְנָה: יְיָ, מִי כָמוֹךָ, מַצִּיל עָנִי מֵחָזָק מִמֶּנּוּ, וְעָנִי וְאֶבְיוֹן מִגֹּזְלוֹ! מִי יִדְמֶה לָּךְ? וּמִי יִשְׁוֶה לָּךְ? וּמִי יַעֲרָךְ לָךְ? הָאֵל הַגָּדוֹל, הַגִּבּוֹר וְהַנּוֹרָא, אֵל עֶלְיוֹן, קוֹנֵה שָׁמַיִם וָאָרֶץ. נְהַלֶּלְךָ, וּנְשַׁבֵּחֲךָ, וּנְפָאֶרְךָ, וּנְבָרֵךְ אֶת שֵׁם קָדְשֶׁךָ, כָּאָמוּר: לְדָוִד, בָּרְכִי נַפְשִׁי אֶת יְיָ, וְכָל קְרָבַי אֶת שֵׁם קָדְשׁוֹ.

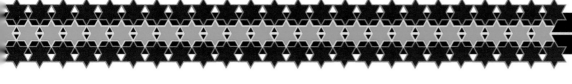

All my bones will say: 'God, who is like You?' You save the poor man from those who are stronger, the poor and needy from robbers. Who is like You? Who is equal to You? Who can be compared to You? O great, mighty, and awesome God, supreme God, Maker of heaven and earth. We will praise, recognize, and glorify You and bless Your holy Name, just as it says: A Psalm of David: Bless God, O my soul, and let my whole inner being bless His holy Name!

הָאֵל בְּתַעֲצֻמוֹת עֻזֶּךָ, הַגָּדוֹל בִּכְבוֹד שְׁמֶךָ, הַגִּבּוֹר לָנֶצַח וְהַנּוֹרָא בְּנוֹרְאוֹתֶיךָ, הַמֶּלֶךְ הַיּוֹשֵׁב עַל כִּסֵּא רָם וְנִשָּׂא.

O God in the power of Your strength, great in the honor of Your name, powerful forever and awesome through Your awesome deeds, O King sitting upon a high and lofty throne!

שׁוֹכֵן עַד, מָרוֹם וְקָדוֹשׁ שְׁמוֹ. וְכָתוּב: רַנְּנוּ צַדִּיקִים בַּיְיָ, לַיְשָׁרִים נָאוָה תְהִלָּה. בְּפִי יְשָׁרִים תִּתְהַלָּל, וּבְדִבְרֵי צַדִּיקִים תִּתְבָּרַךְ, וּבִלְשׁוֹן חֲסִידִים תִּתְרוֹמָם, וּבְקֶרֶב קְדוֹשִׁים תִּתְקַדָּשׁ.

He Who remains forever, respected and holy is His Name. And it says: Those who are good, be happy in God; for to them, His praise is pleasant. The proud will praise You; the good will bless You; the devoted will respect you; and the holy will cherish You.

וּבְמַקְהֲלוֹת רִבְבוֹת עַמְּךָ בֵּית יִשְׂרָאֵל בְּרִנָּה יִתְפָּאַר שִׁמְךָ, מַלְכֵּנוּ, בְּכָל דּוֹר וָדוֹר, שֶׁכֵּן חוֹבַת כָּל הַיְצוּרִים לְפָנֶיךָ, יְיָ אֱלֹהֵינוּ וֵאלֹהֵי אֲבוֹתֵינוּ, לְהוֹדוֹת, לְהַלֵּל, לְשַׁבֵּחַ, לְפָאֵר, לְרוֹמֵם, לְהַדֵּר, לְבָרֵךְ, לְעַלֵּה וּלְקַלֵּס, עַל כָּל דִּבְרֵי שִׁירוֹת וְתִשְׁבְּחוֹת דָּוִד בֶּן יִשַׁי עַבְדְּךָ מְשִׁיחֶךָ.

And throughout Your many people of Israel, Your name, our King, will be honored with happiness in every generation. For that is the job of all living things — in front of You, God, and God of our ancestors, to thank, praise, compliment, glorify, honor, adore, bless, raise high, and sing praises — even more than the songs and praises of David the son of Jesse, Your servant, Your chosen.

יִשְׁתַּבַּח שִׁמְךָ לָעַד מַלְכֵּנוּ,
הָאֵל, הַמֶּלֶךְ הַגָּדוֹל וְהַקָּדוֹשׁ
בַּשָּׁמַיִם וּבָאָרֶץ, כִּי לְךָ נָאֶה,
יְיָ אֱלֹהֵינוּ וֵאלֹהֵי אֲבוֹתֵינוּ,
שִׁיר וּשְׁבָחָה. הַלֵּל וְזִמְרָה.
עֹז וּמֶמְשָׁלָה, נֶצַח גְּדֻלָּה
וּגְבוּרָה, תְּהִלָּה וְתִפְאֶרֶת,
קְדֻשָּׁה וּמַלְכוּת, בְּרָכוֹת
וְהוֹדָאוֹת, מֵעַתָּה וְעַד עוֹלָם.
בָּרוּךְ אַתָּה יְיָ, אֵל מֶלֶךְ גָּדוֹל
בַּתִּשְׁבָּחוֹת, אֵל הַהוֹדָאוֹת,
אֲדוֹן הַנִּפְלָאוֹת, הַבּוֹחֵר
בְּשִׁירֵי זִמְרָה, מֶלֶךְ אֵל חֵי
הָעוֹלָמִים.

May Your Name be praised forever, our King, the God and King Who is great and holy in heaven and on earth; for to You, God and God of our ancestors, it is proper to sing and praise, hallel and hymns, power and dominion, victory, greatness and might, praise and glory, holiness and power, blessings and thanksgiving, from now and forever. Blessed are You, God, King, great in praises, God of thanksgiving, Master of wonders, Who favors songs of praise — King, God, Life of all worlds.

The Haggadah Story

• The Exodus from Egypt was the start of the Jewish people as a nation. It is mentioned in the Torah 160 times, showing the importance of Pesach. There are 36 mitzvot for Pesach and another 31 directly related to the holiday —that's almost 10% of all mitzvot!

• Since the exodus from Egypt, the story has been told from father to son, from family to family, and from one generation to the next — until it reached us!

• Rabbi Shlomo Goren put together a special Haggadah for the Israel Defense Forces, combining Ashkenazi, Sephardi, Yemenite and other traditions.

• As early as 500 B.C.E., a Daryush Jewish soldier wrote a letter on papyrus discussing preparations for the holiday.

• The first Pesach in Canaan, was celebrated by Joshua and his army. (Exodus 5: 10-12).

בָּרוּךְ אַתָּה יְיָ, אֱלֹהֵינוּ מֶלֶךְ הָעוֹלָם, בּוֹרֵא פְּרִי הַגָּפֶן.

Drink the fourth cup while leaning to the left side.

בָּרוּךְ אַתָּה יְיָ, אֱלֹהֵינוּ מֶלֶךְ הָעוֹלָם, עַל הַגֶּפֶן וְעַל פְּרִי הַגֶּפֶן, וְעַל תְּנוּבַת הַשָּׂדֶה,
וְעַל אֶרֶץ חֶמְדָּה טוֹבָה וּרְחָבָה, שֶׁרָצִיתָ וְהִנְחַלְתָּ לַאֲבוֹתֵינוּ, לֶאֱכוֹל מִפִּרְיָהּ
וְלִשְׂבּוֹעַ מִטּוּבָהּ. רַחֶם נָא יְיָ אֱלֹהֵינוּ עַל יִשְׂרָאֵל עַמֶּךָ, וְעַל יְרוּשָׁלַיִם עִירֶךָ, וְעַל
צִיּוֹן מִשְׁכַּן כְּבוֹדֶךָ, וְעַל מִזְבְּחֶךָ וְעַל הֵיכָלֶךָ. וּבְנֵה יְרוּשָׁלַיִם עִיר הַקֹּדֶשׁ בִּמְהֵרָה
בְיָמֵינוּ. וְהַעֲלֵנוּ לְתוֹכָהּ וְשַׂמְּחֵנוּ בְּבִנְיָנָהּ וְנֹאכַל מִפִּרְיָהּ וְנִשְׂבַּע מִטּוּבָהּ וּנְבָרֶכְךָ
עָלֶיהָ בִּקְדֻשָּׁה וּבְטָהֳרָה. (*On the Sabbath* וּרְצֵה וְהַחֲלִיצֵנוּ בְּיוֹם הַשַּׁבָּת הַזֶּה) וְשַׂמְּחֵנוּ
בְּיוֹם חַג הַמַּצּוֹת הַזֶּה, כִּי אַתָּה יְיָ טוֹב וּמֵטִיב לַכֹּל; וְנוֹדֶה לְךָ עַל הָאָרֶץ וְעַל
פְּרִי הַגָּפֶן. בָּרוּךְ אַתָּה יְיָ, עַל הָאָרֶץ וְעַל פְּרִי הַגָּפֶן.

Blessed are You, God, King of the universe, Who creates the fruit of the vine.

Blessed are You, God, King of the universe, for the vine and the fruit of the vine, and for the produce of the field. For the valuable, good, and spacious land that You gave our ancestors as a heritage, to eat its fruit and to be satisfied with its goodness. Have mercy, we beg You, God, on Israel Your people; on Jerusalem, Your city; on Zion, resting place of Your glory; Your altar, and Your Temple. Rebuild Jerusalem, the holy city, quickly in our time. Bring us to it and make us happy by rebuilding it and let us eat from its fruit and be satisfied with its goodness and bless You in it in holiness and purity. (*On the Sabbath.* Favor us and make us strong on this Sabbath day) and give us happiness on this Festival of Matzos; for You, God, are good and do good to all, and we thank You for the land and for the fruit of the vine. Blessed are You, God, for the land and for the fruit of the vine.

נִרְצָה

CONCLUSION OF THE SEDER

חֲסַל סִדּוּר פֶּסַח כְּהִלְכָתוֹ, כְּכָל מִשְׁפָּטוֹ וְחֻקָּתוֹ.
כַּאֲשֶׁר זָכִינוּ לְסַדֵּר אוֹתוֹ, כֵּן נִזְכֶּה לַעֲשׂוֹתוֹ.

We have now finished the Seder with all its laws and rulings. Just as we were honored to put it together, we are also honored to carry it out.

זָךְ שׁוֹכֵן מְעוֹנָה, קוֹמֵם קְהַל עֲדַת מִי מָנָה.
בְּקָרוֹב נַהֵל נִטְעֵי כַנָּה, פְּדוּיִם לְצִיּוֹן בְּרִנָּה.

O Pure One, Who is so holy, raise up the many communities, soon — lead the offshoots of Your plants, rescued, to Zion with happiness.

לשנה הבאה בירושלים
Next Year In Jerusalem

Holiday Hymns for Passover

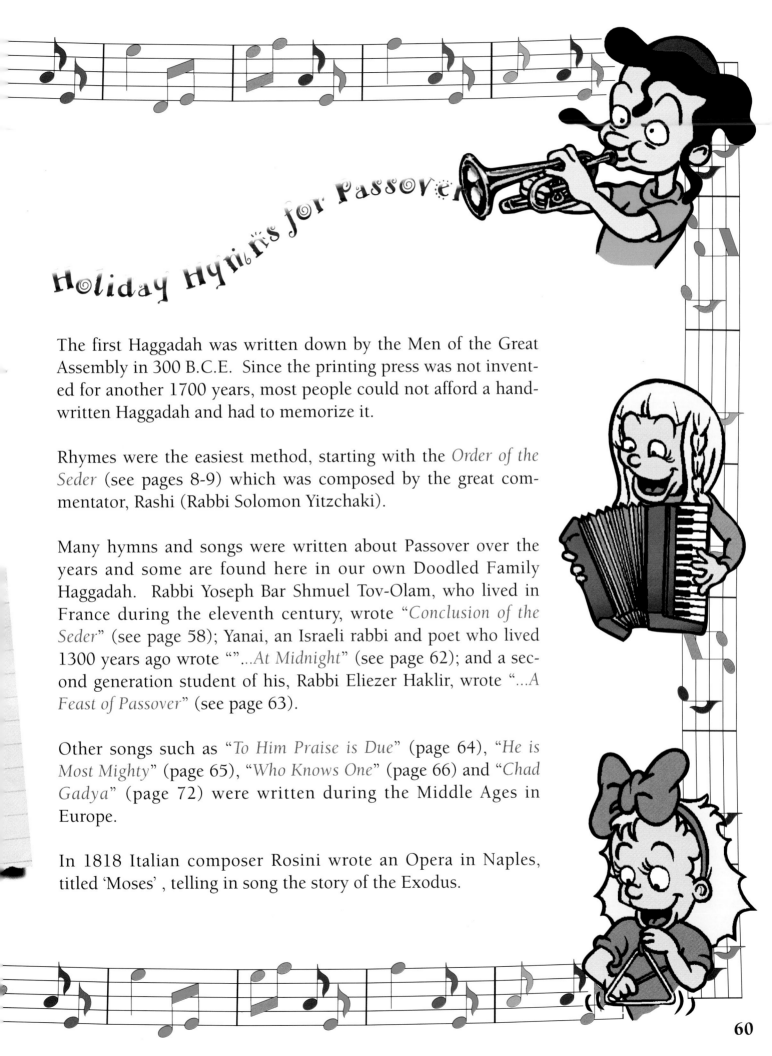

The first Haggadah was written down by the Men of the Great Assembly in 300 B.C.E. Since the printing press was not invented for another 1700 years, most people could not afford a handwritten Haggadah and had to memorize it.

Rhymes were the easiest method, starting with the *Order of the Seder* (see pages 8-9) which was composed by the great commentator, Rashi (Rabbi Solomon Yitzchaki).

Many hymns and songs were written about Passover over the years and some are found here in our own Doodled Family Haggadah. Rabbi Yoseph Bar Shmuel Tov-Olam, who lived in France during the eleventh century, wrote "*Conclusion of the Seder*" (see page 58); Yanai, an Israeli rabbi and poet who lived 1300 years ago wrote ""*...At Midnight*" (see page 62); and a second generation student of his, Rabbi Eliezer Haklir, wrote "*...A Feast of Passover*" (see page 63).

Other songs such as "*To Him Praise is Due*" (page 64), "*He is Most Mighty*" (page 65), "*Who Knows One*" (page 66) and "*Chad Gadya*" (page 72) were written during the Middle Ages in Europe.

In 1818 Italian composer Rosini wrote an Opera in Naples, titled 'Moses' , telling in song the story of the Exodus.

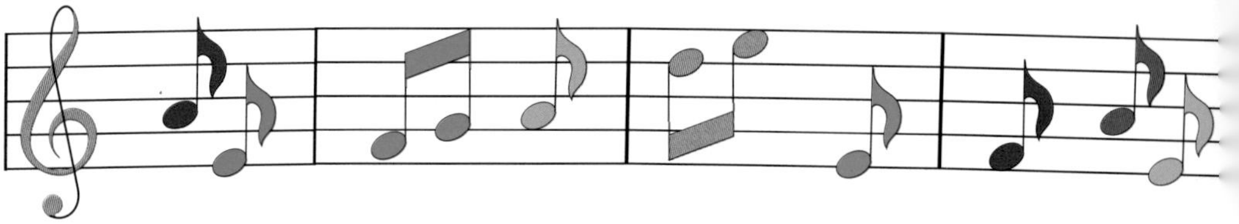

OUR UNCLE YANKEL CALLED TO SAY
HE'LL COME DOWN FOR THE SEDER
"I'LL BRING SOME MATZAHS AND SOME WINE -
GOOD-BYE, I'LL SEE YOU LATER!"

YANKEL DOODLE RODE TO TOWN
IN HIS PILE OF RUST
HE TURNED LEFT (HE SHOULDN'T HAVE!)
HIS MATZAHS TURNED TO DUST.

A BEARDED STRANGER, WHITE AND TALL,
REMOVED HIM FROM THE WRECK
TOGETHER SWIGGING MANISCHEWITZ
THEY MADE A HOME-BOUND TREK.

AND MEANWHILE AT THE SEDER FEAST
WE POURED CUP NUMBER FOUR
WE POURED OUR WRATH, WE POURED OUR RAGE,
WE OPENED WIDE OUR DOOR.

AND AT THAT MOMENT, LIMPING IN,
OUR UNCLE AND HIS MATE,
APPROACHED THE TABLE AND YANKEL SAID;
"SO SORRY THAT I'M LATE."

THE STRANGER REACHED FOR ELIJAH'S CUP
HIS EYES A FIERY LIGHT
HE GULPED IT DOWN, THEN TURNED AROUND
AND VANISHED IN THE NIGHT.

AND TO THIS DAY OUR UNCLE SWEARS
HIS SAVIOR WAS THE PROPHET
BUT ZAIDY SAYS "YOU MUST BE NUTS
HE'S JUST SOME DRUNK, GET OFF IT!"

NOW EVERY YEAR WE OPEN DOOR
WHEN SEDER COMES AROUND
OUR POODLE'S HOWL WILL PIERCE THE NIGHT
LIKE A MIGHTY SHOFAR SOUND.

*The Doodle Famil
also has their owr
Passover ballad,
which they sing
to the tune of
"Yankee Doodle."*

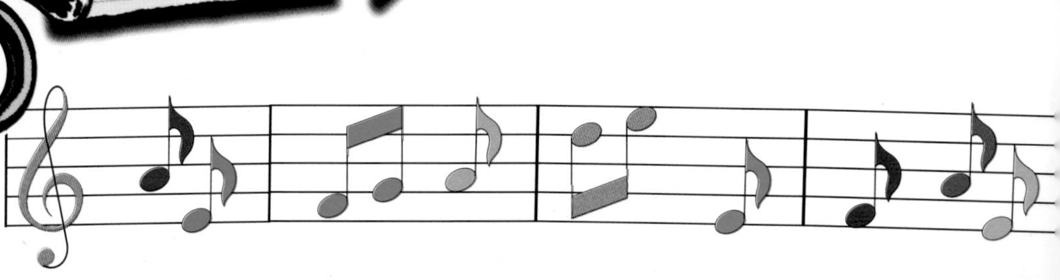

On the first Seder night say:

IT HAPPENED AT MIDNIGHT.

You have, in the past, performed many wonders at night, At the head of the watches of this night, To the righteous convert (Abraham), You gave triumph by dividing for him the night,

It happened at midnight.

You judged the king of Gerar (Abimelech), in a dream by night, You frightened the Aramean (Laban), in the dark of night. And Israel overcame the angel at night.

It happened at midnight.

Egypt's first-born, you crushed at midnight, Their host they didn't find when arising at night. The army of the prince of Charoshes (Sisera) You swept away with stars of the night.

It happened at midnight.

The blasphemer (Sennacherib), planned to raise his hand against Jerusalem— but You withered his corpses by night. Bel was overturned with its pedestal, in the darkness of night. To the man of Your delights (Daniel), was revealed the mystery of the visions of night.

It happened at midnight.

He (Belshazzar) who drank from the holy vessels was killed that very night. From the lions den was rescued he (Daniel) who interpreted the terrors of the night. The Aggagite (Haman) became hateful and wrote decrees at night.

It happened at midnight.

You began Your triumph over him when You disturbed (Ahasverus') sleep at night. Trample the wine-press to help those who ask the watchman, "what of the long night?" He will shout, like a watchman, and say: "Morning shall come after night."

It happened at midnight.

Hasten the day (of Messiah), that is neither day nor night. Appoint guards for Your city, all the day and all the night Brighten like the light of day the darkness of night.

IT HAPPENED AT MIDNIGHT.

וַיְהִי בַּחֲצִי הַלַּיְלָה.

אָז רוֹב נִסִּים הִפְלֵאתָ בַּלַּיְלָה, בְּרֹאשׁ אַשְׁמוּרוֹת זֶה הַלַּיְלָה, גֵּר צֶדֶק נִצַּחְתּוֹ כְּנֶחֱלַק לוֹ לַיְלָה,

וַיְהִי בַּחֲצִי הַלַּיְלָה.

דַּנְתָּ מֶלֶךְ גְּרָר בַּחֲלוֹם הַלַּיְלָה, הִפְחַדְתָּ אֲרַמִּי בְּאֶמֶשׁ לַיְלָה, וַיָּשַׂר יִשְׂרָאֵל לְמַלְאָךְ וַיּוּכַל לוֹ לַיְלָה,

וַיְהִי בַּחֲצִי הַלַּיְלָה.

זֶרַע בְּכוֹרֵי פַתְרוֹס מָחַצְתָּ בַּחֲצִי הַלַּיְלָה, חֵילָם לֹא מָצְאוּ בְּקוּמָם בַּלַּיְלָה, טִיסַת נְגִיד חֲרֹשֶׁת סִלִּיתָ בְכוֹכְבֵי לַיְלָה,

וַיְהִי בַּחֲצִי הַלַּיְלָה.

יָעַץ מְחָרֵף לְנוֹפֵף אִוּוּי, הוֹבַשְׁתָּ פְגָרָיו בַּלַּיְלָה, כָּרַע בֵּל וּמַצָּבוֹ בְּאִישׁוֹן לַיְלָה, לְאִישׁ חֲמוּדוֹת נִגְלָה רָז חֲזוֹת לַיְלָה,

וַיְהִי בַּחֲצִי הַלַּיְלָה.

מִשְׁתַּכֵּר בִּכְלֵי קֹדֶשׁ נֶהֱרַג בּוֹ בַּלַּיְלָה, נוֹשַׁע מִבּוֹר אֲרָיוֹת פּוֹתֵר בִּעוּתֵי לַיְלָה. שִׂנְאָה נָטַר אֲגָגִי וְכָתַב סְפָרִים בַּלַּיְלָה,

וַיְהִי בַּחֲצִי הַלַּיְלָה.

עוֹרַרְתָּ נִצְחֲךָ עָלָיו בְּנֶדֶד שְׁנַת לַיְלָה, פּוּרָה תִדְרוֹךְ לְשׁוֹמֵר מַה מִּלַּיְלָה, צָרַח כַּשּׁוֹמֵר וְשָׂח אָתָא בֹקֶר וְגַם לַיְלָה,

וַיְהִי בַּחֲצִי הַלַּיְלָה.

קָרֵב יוֹם אֲשֶׁר הוּא לֹא יוֹם וְלֹא לַיְלָה, רָם הוֹדַע כִּי לְךָ הַיּוֹם אַף לְךָ הַלַּיְלָה, שׁוֹמְרִים הַפְקֵד לְעִירְךָ כָּל הַיּוֹם וְכָל הַלַּיְלָה, תָּאִיר כְּאוֹר יוֹם חֶשְׁכַת לַיְלָה,

וַיְהִי בַּחֲצִי הַלַּיְלָה.

"...By night in a pillar of fire, to give light to them."

Exodus 13:21

AND YOU SHOULD SAY: A FEAST OF PASSOVER.

You displayed wondrously Your mighty powers on Passover. Above all festivals You elevated Passover. To the Oriental (Abraham) You revealed the future midnight of Passover.

And you should say: A feast of Passover.

At his door You knocked in the heat of the day on Passover; He satiated the angels with matzah-cakes on Passover And he ran to the hear—symbolic of the sacrificial beast of Passover.

And you should say: A feast of Passover.

The Sodomites provoked (God) and were devoured by fire on Passover; Lot was withdrawn from them — he had baked matzot at the time of Passover. You swept clean the soil of Moph and Noph (in Egypt) when You passed through on Passover.

And you should say: A feast of Passover.

God, You crushed every first-born of On (in Egypt) on the watchful night of Passover.
But Master — Your own first-born, You skipped by merit of the blood of Passover.
Not to allow the Destroyer to enter my doors on Passover.

And you should say: A feast of Passover.

The surrounded (Jericho) was attacked on Passover. Midian was destroyed with a barley cake, from the Omer of Passover. The mighty nobles of Pul and Lud (Assyria) were consumed in a great fire on Passover.

And you should say: A feast of Passover.

He (Sennacherib) would have stood that day at Nob, but for the coming of Passover. A hand wrote the destruction of Zul (Babylon) on Passover. As the watch was fixed, and the royal table set on Passover.

And you should say: A feast of Passover.

Hadassah (Esther) gathered a congregation for a three-day fast on Passover. You caused the head of the evil clan (Haman) to be hanged on a fifty-cubit gallows on Passover; Let Your hand be strong, and Your right arm made holy,
as on that night when You made special the festival of Passover.

AND YOU SHOULD SAY: A FEAST OF PASSOVER.

וַאֲמַרְתֶּם זֶבַח פֶּסַח.

אֹמֶץ גְּבוּרוֹתֶיךָ הִפְלֵאתָ בַּפֶּסַח,
בְּרֹאשׁ כָּל מוֹעֲדוֹת נִשֵּׂאתָ פֶּסַח,
גִּלִּיתָ לָאֶזְרָחִי חֲצוֹת לֵיל פֶּסַח,

וַאֲמַרְתֶּם זֶבַח פֶּסַח.

דְּלָתָיו דָּפַקְתָּ כְּחֹם הַיּוֹם בַּפֶּסַח, הִסְעִיד נוֹצְצִים עֻגוֹת מַצּוֹת בַּפֶּסַח, וְאֶל הַבָּקָר רָץ זֵכֶר לְשׁוֹר עֵרֶךְ פֶּסַח,

וַאֲמַרְתֶּם זֶבַח פֶּסַח.

זֹעֲמוּ סְדוֹמִים וְלֹהֲטוּ בָּאֵשׁ בַּפֶּסַח, חֻלַּץ לוֹט מֵהֶם, וּמַצּוֹת אָפָה בְּקֵץ פֶּסַח, טִאטֵאתָ אַדְמַת מֹף וְנֹף בְּעָבְרְךָ בַּפֶּסַח,

וַאֲמַרְתֶּם זֶבַח פֶּסַח.

יָהּ, רֹאשׁ כָּל אוֹן מָחַצְתָּ בְּלֵיל שִׁמּוּר פֶּסַח, כַּבִּיר, עַל בֵּן בְּכוֹר פָּסַחְתָּ בְּדַם פֶּסַח, לְבִלְתִּי תֵּת מַשְׁחִית לָבֹא בִּפְתָחַי בַּפֶּסַח,

וַאֲמַרְתֶּם זֶבַח פֶּסַח.

מְסֻגֶּרֶת סֻגָּרָה בְּעִתּוֹתֵי פֶּסַח, נִשְׁמְדָה מִדְיָן בִּצְלִיל שְׂעוֹרֵי עֹמֶר פֶּסַח, שׂוֹרְפוּ מִשְׁמַנֵּי פּוּל וְלוּד בִּיקַד יְקוֹד פֶּסַח,

וַאֲמַרְתֶּם זֶבַח פֶּסַח.

עוֹד הַיּוֹם בְּנֹב לַעֲמֹד, עַד גָּעָה עוֹנַת פֶּסַח, פַּס יָד כָּתְבָה לְקַעֲקֵעַ צוּל בַּפֶּסַח, צָפֹה הַצָּפִית עָרוֹךְ הַשֻּׁלְחָן, בַּפֶּסַח,

וַאֲמַרְתֶּם זֶבַח פֶּסַח.

קָהָל כִּנְּסָה הֲדַסָּה לְשַׁלֵּשׁ צוֹם בַּפֶּסַח, רֹאשׁ מִבֵּית רָשָׁע מָחַצְתָּ בְּעֵץ חֲמִשִּׁים בַּפֶּסַח, שְׁתֵּי אֵלֶּה רֶגַע, תָּבִיא לְעוּצִית בַּפֶּסַח, תָּעֹז יָדְךָ תָּרוּם יְמִינְךָ, כְּלֵיל הִתְקַדֵּשׁ חַג פֶּסַח,

וַאֲמַרְתֶּם זֶבַח פֶּסַח.

"...By day in a pillar of cloud, to lead them the way."

Exodus 13:21

כִּי לוֹ נָאֶה, כִּי לוֹ יָאֶה.

אַדִּיר בִּמְלוּכָה, בָּחוּר כַּהֲלָכָה, גְּדוּדָיו יֹאמְרוּ לוֹ: לְךָ
וּלְךָ, לְךָ כִּי לְךָ, לְךָ אַף לְךָ, לְךָ יְיָ הַמַּמְלָכָה.
כִּי לוֹ נָאֶה, כִּי לוֹ יָאֶה.
דָּגוּל בִּמְלוּכָה, הָדוּר כַּהֲלָכָה, וָתִיקָיו יֹאמְרוּ לוֹ: לְךָ
וּלְךָ, לְךָ כִּי לְךָ, לְךָ אַף לְךָ, לְךָ יְיָ הַמַּמְלָכָה.
כִּי לוֹ נָאֶה, כִּי לוֹ יָאֶה.
זַכַּאי בִּמְלוּכָה, חָסִין כַּהֲלָכָה, טַפְסְרָיו יֹאמְרוּ לוֹ: לְךָ
וּלְךָ, לְךָ כִּי לְךָ, לְךָ אַף לְךָ, לְךָ יְיָ הַמַּמְלָכָה.
כִּי לוֹ נָאֶה, כִּי לוֹ יָאֶה.
יָחִיד בִּמְלוּכָה, כַּבִּיר כַּהֲלָכָה, לִמּוּדָיו יֹאמְרוּ לוֹ: לְךָ
וּלְךָ, לְךָ כִּי לְךָ, לְךָ אַף לְךָ, לְךָ יְיָ הַמַּמְלָכָה.
כִּי לוֹ נָאֶה, כִּי לוֹ יָאֶה.
מוֹשֵׁל בִּמְלוּכָה, נוֹרָא כַּהֲלָכָה, סְבִיבָיו יֹאמְרוּ לוֹ: לְךָ
וּלְךָ, לְךָ כִּי לְךָ, לְךָ אַף לְךָ, לְךָ יְיָ הַמַּמְלָכָה.
כִּי לוֹ נָאֶה, כִּי לוֹ יָאֶה.
עָנָו בִּמְלוּכָה, פּוֹדֶה כַּהֲלָכָה, צַדִּיקָיו יֹאמְרוּ לוֹ: לְךָ
וּלְךָ, לְךָ כִּי לְךָ, לְךָ אַף לְךָ, לְךָ יְיָ הַמַּמְלָכָה.
כִּי לוֹ נָאֶה, כִּי לוֹ יָאֶה.
קָדוֹשׁ בִּמְלוּכָה, רַחוּם כַּהֲלָכָה, שִׁנְאַנָּיו יֹאמְרוּ לוֹ:
לְךָ וּלְךָ, לְךָ כִּי לְךָ, לְךָ אַף לְךָ, לְךָ יְיָ הַמַּמְלָכָה.
כִּי לוֹ נָאֶה, כִּי לוֹ יָאֶה.
תַּקִּיף בִּמְלוּכָה, תּוֹמֵךְ כַּהֲלָכָה, תְּמִימָיו יֹאמְרוּ לוֹ:
לְךָ וּלְךָ, לְךָ כִּי לְךָ, לְךָ אַף לְךָ, לְךָ יְיָ הַמַּמְלָכָה.
כִּי לוֹ נָאֶה, כִּי לוֹ יָאֶה.

אַדִּיר הוּא

יִבְנֶה בֵיתוֹ בְּקָרוֹב, בִּמְהֵרָה בִּמְהֵרָה, בְּיָמֵינוּ בְּקָרוֹב.
אֵל בְּנֵה, אֵל בְּנֵה, בְּנֵה בֵיתְךָ בְּקָרוֹב.
בָּחוּר הוּא, גָּדוֹל הוּא, דָּגוּל הוּא, יִבְנֶה בֵיתוֹ
בְּקָרוֹב, בִּמְהֵרָה בִּמְהֵרָה, בְּיָמֵינוּ בְּקָרוֹב.
אֵל בְּנֵה, אֵל בְּנֵה, בְּנֵה בֵיתְךָ בְּקָרוֹב.
הָדוּר הוּא, וָתִיק הוּא, זַכַּאי הוּא, חָסִיד הוּא,
יִבְנֶה בֵיתוֹ בְּקָרוֹב, בִּמְהֵרָה בִּמְהֵרָה, בְּיָמֵינוּ בְּקָרוֹב.
אֵל בְּנֵה, אֵל בְּנֵה, בְּנֵה בֵיתְךָ בְּקָרוֹב.
טָהוֹר הוּא, יָחִיד הוּא, כַּבִּיר הוּא, לָמוּד הוּא,
מֶלֶךְ הוּא, נוֹרָא הוּא סַגִּיב הוּא, עִזּוּז הוּא, פּוֹדֶה
הוּא, צַדִּיק הוּא, יִבְנֶה בֵיתוֹ בְּקָרוֹב, בִּמְהֵרָה
בִּמְהֵרָה, בְּיָמֵינוּ בְּקָרוֹב.
אֵל בְּנֵה, אֵל בְּנֵה, בְּנֵה בֵיתְךָ בְּקָרוֹב.
קָדוֹשׁ הוּא, רַחוּם הוּא, שַׁדַּי הוּא, תַּקִּיף הוּא,
יִבְנֶה בֵיתוֹ בְּקָרוֹב, בִּמְהֵרָה בִּמְהֵרָה, בְּיָמֵינוּ בְּקָרוֹב.
אֵל בְּנֵה, אֵל בְּנֵה, בְּנֵה בֵיתְךָ בְּקָרוֹב.

TO HIM PRAISE IS DUE! TO HIM PRAISE IS FITTING!

Powerful in majesty, perfectly distinguished, His companies of angels say to him: Yours and only Yours; Yours, yes Yours, surely Yours, Yours, God, is the authority.

To Him praise is due! To Him praise is fitting!

Supreme in kingship, perfectly glorious, His faithful say to Him: Yours and only Yours; Yours, yes Yours; Yours, surely Yours; Yours, God, is the authority.

To Him praise is due! To Him praise is fitting!

Pure in kingship, perfectly mighty, His angels say to him: Yours and only Yours; Yours, yes Yours; Yours, surely Yours; Yours, God, is the authority.

To Him praise is due! To Him praise is fitting.

Alone in kingship, perfectly all-powerful, His scholars say to Him: Yours and only Yours; Yours, yes Yours; Yours, surely Yours; Yours, God, is the authority.

To Him praise is due! To Him praise is fitting!

Commanding in kingship, perfectly wondrous, His surrounding (angels) say to Him: Yours and only Yours, Yours, yes Yours; Yours, surely Yours; Yours, God, is the authority.

To Him praise is due! To Him praise is fitting!

Gentle in Kingship, perfectly the Redeemer, His righteous say to Him: Yours and only Yours; Yours, yes Yours; Yours, surely Yours; Yours, God, is the authority.

To Him praise is due! To Him praise is fitting!

Holy in kingship, perfectly merciful, His troops of angels say to Him: Yours and only Yours; Yours, yes Yours; Yours, surely Yours; Yours, God, is the authority.

To Him praise is due! To Him praise is fitting!

Almighty in kingship, perfectly sustaining, His perfect ones say to Him: Yours and only Yours; Yours, yes Yours; Yours, surely Yours; Yours, God, is the authority.

To Him praise is due! To Him praise is fitting!

HE IS MOST MIGHTY

May He soon rebuild His House, speedily, yes speedily, in our days, soon.

God, rebuild, God, rebuild, rebuild Your House soon!

He is distinguished, He is great, He is raised up. May He soon rebuild His House, speedily, yes speedily, in our days, soon.

God, rebuild, God, rebuild, rebuild Your House soon!

He is all glorious, He is faithful, He is faultless, He is righteous. May He soon rebuild His House, speedily, yes speedily, in our days, soon.

God, rebuild, God, rebuild, rebuild Your House soon!

He is pure, He is unique, He is powerful, He is all-wise, He is King, He is awesome, He is virtuous, He is all-powerful, He is the Redeemer, He is the all-righteous. May He soon rebuild His House, speedily, yes speedily, in our days, soon.

God, rebuild, God, rebuild, rebuild Your House soon!

He is holy, He is compassionate, He is Almighty, He is omnipotent. May He soon rebuild His House, speedily, yes speedily, in our days, soon.

God, rebuild, God, rebuild, rebuild Your House soon!

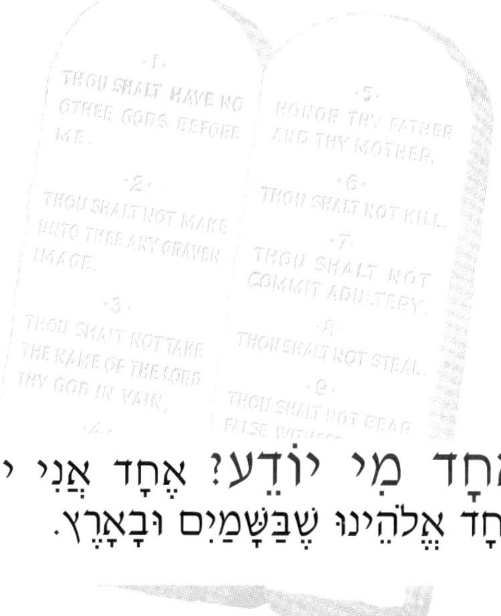

אֶחָד מִי יוֹדֵעַ? אֶחָד אֲנִי יוֹדֵעַ: אֶחָד אֱלֹהֵינוּ שֶׁבַּשָּׁמַיִם וּבָאָרֶץ.

WHO KNOWS ONE? I know one: One is our God, in heaven and on earth.

שְׁנַיִם מִי יוֹדֵעַ? שְׁנַיִם אֲנִי יוֹדֵעַ: שְׁנֵי לֻחוֹת הַבְּרִית, אֶחָד אֱלֹהֵינוּ שֶׁבַּשָּׁמַיִם וּבָאָרֶץ.

WHO KNOWS TWO? I know two: two are the Tablets of the Covenant; One is our God, in heaven and on earth.

שְׁלֹשָׁה מִי יוֹדֵעַ? שְׁלֹשָׁה אֲנִי יוֹדֵעַ: שְׁלֹשָׁה אָבוֹת, שְׁנֵי לֻחוֹת הַבְּרִית, אֶחָד אֱלֹהֵינוּ שֶׁבַּשָּׁמַיִם וּבָאָרֶץ.

WHO KNOWS THREE? I know three: three are the Patriarchs; two are the Tablets of the Covenant; One is our God, in heaven and on earth.

אַרְבַּע מִי יוֹדֵעַ? אַרְבַּע אֲנִי יוֹדֵעַ: אַרְבַּע אִמָּהוֹת, שְׁלֹשָׁה אָבוֹת, שְׁנֵי לֻחוֹת הַבְּרִית, אֶחָד אֱלֹהֵינוּ שֶׁבַּשָּׁמַיִם וּבָאָרֶץ.

WHO KNOWS FOUR? I know four: four are the Matriarchs; three are the Patriarchs; two are the Tablets of the Covenant; One is our God, in heaven and on earth.

WHO KNOWS FIVE? I know five: five are the books of Torah; four are the Matriarchs; three are the Patriarchs; two are the Tablets of the Covenant; One is our God, in heaven and on earth.

חֲמִשָּׁה מִי יוֹדֵעַ? חֲמִשָּׁה אֲנִי יוֹדֵעַ:
חֲמִשָּׁה חוּמְשֵׁי תוֹרָה, אַרְבַּע אִמָּהוֹת,
שְׁלֹשָׁה אָבוֹת, שְׁנֵי לֻחוֹת הַבְּרִית, אֶחָד
אֱלֹהֵינוּ שֶׁבַּשָּׁמַיִם וּבָאָרֶץ.

WHO KNOWS SIX? I know six: six are the Orders of the Mishnah; five are the books of Torah; four are the Matriarchs; three are the Patriarchs; two are the Tablets of the Covenant; One is our God, in heaven and on earth.

שִׁשָּׁה מִי יוֹדֵעַ? שִׁשָּׁה אֲנִי יוֹדֵעַ:
שִׁשָּׁה סִדְרֵי מִשְׁנָה, חֲמִשָּׁה חוּמְשֵׁי תוֹרָה,
אַרְבַּע אִמָּהוֹת, שְׁלֹשָׁה אָבוֹת, שְׁנֵי לֻחוֹת
הַבְּרִית, אֶחָד אֱלֹהֵינוּ שֶׁבַּשָּׁמַיִם וּבָאָרֶץ:

WHO KNOWS SEVEN? I know seven: seven are the days of the week; six are the Orders of the Mishnah; five are the books of the Torah; four are the Matriarchs; three are the Patriarchs; two are the Tablets of the Covenant; One is our God, in heaven and on earth.

שִׁבְעָה מִי יוֹדֵעַ? שִׁבְעָה אֲנִי יוֹדֵעַ:
שִׁבְעָה יְמֵי שַׁבְּתָא, שִׁשָּׁה סִדְרֵי מִשְׁנָה,
חֲמִשָּׁה חוּמְשֵׁי תוֹרָה, אַרְבַּע אִמָּהוֹת,
שְׁלֹשָׁה אָבוֹת, שְׁנֵי לֻחוֹת הַבְּרִית, אֶחָד
אֱלֹהֵינוּ שֶׁבַּשָּׁמַיִם וּבָאָרֶץ.

WHO KNOWS EIGHT? I know eight: eight are the days of circumcision; seven are the days of the week; six are the Orders of the Mishnah; five are the books of Torah; four are the Matriarchs; three are the Patriarchs; two are the Tablets of the Covenant; One is our God, in heaven and on earth.

שְׁמוֹנָה מִי יוֹדֵעַ? שְׁמוֹנָה אֲנִי יוֹדֵעַ:
שְׁמוֹנָה יְמֵי מִילָה, שִׁבְעָה יְמֵי שַׁבְּתָא,
שִׁשָּׁה סִדְרֵי מִשְׁנָה, חֲמִשָּׁה חוּמְשֵׁי תוֹרָה,
אַרְבַּע אִמָּהוֹת, שְׁלֹשָׁה אָבוֹת, שְׁנֵי לֻחוֹת
הַבְּרִית, אֶחָד אֱלֹהֵינוּ שֶׁבַּשָּׁמַיִם וּבָאָרֶץ.

WHO KNOWS NINE? I know nine: nine are the months of pregnancy; eight are the days of circumcision; seven are the days of the week; six are the Orders of the Mishnah; five are the books of the Torah; four are the Matriarchs; three are the Patriarchs; two are the Tablets of the Covenant; One is our God, in heaven and on the earth.

תִּשְׁעָה מִי יוֹדֵעַ? תִּשְׁעָה אֲנִי יוֹדֵעַ:
תִּשְׁעָה יַרְחֵי לֵדָה, שְׁמוֹנָה יְמֵי מִילָה,
שִׁבְעָה יְמֵי שַׁבְּתָא, שִׁשָּׁה סִדְרֵי מִשְׁנָה,
חֲמִשָּׁה חוּמְשֵׁי תוֹרָה, אַרְבַּע אִמָּהוֹת,
שְׁלֹשָׁה אָבוֹת, שְׁנֵי לֻחוֹת הַבְּרִית, אֶחָד
אֱלֹהֵינוּ שֶׁבַּשָּׁמַיִם וּבָאָרֶץ.

WHO KNOWS TEN? I know ten: ten are the Ten Commandments; nine are the months of pregnancy; eight are the days of circumcision; seven are the days of the week; six are the Orders of the Mishnah; five are the books of the Torah; four are the Matriarchs; three are the Patriarchs; two are the Tablets of the Covenant; One is our God, in heaven and on earth.

עֲשָׂרָה מִי יוֹדֵעַ? עֲשָׂרָה אֲנִי יוֹדֵעַ:
עֲשָׂרָה דִבְּרַיָּא, תִּשְׁעָה יַרְחֵי לֵדָה, שְׁמוֹנָה
יְמֵי מִילָה, שִׁבְעָה יְמֵי שַׁבְּתָא, שִׁשָּׁה
סִדְרֵי מִשְׁנָה, חֲמִשָּׁה חוּמְשֵׁי תוֹרָה,
אַרְבַּע אִמָּהוֹת, שְׁלֹשָׁה אָבוֹת, שְׁנֵי לֻחוֹת
הַבְּרִית, אֶחָד אֱלֹהֵינוּ שֶׁבַּשָּׁמַיִם וּבָאָרֶץ.

WHO KNOWS ELEVEN? I know eleven: eleven are the stars (in Joseph's dream); ten are the Ten Commandments; nine are the months of pregnancy; eight are the days of circumcision; seven are the days of the week; six are the Orders of the Mishnah; five are the books of the Torah; four are the Matriarchs; three are the Patriarchs; two are the Tablets of the Covenant; One is our God, in heaven and on earth.

אַחַד עָשָׂר מִי יוֹדֵעַ? אַחַד עָשָׂר
אֲנִי יוֹדֵעַ: אַחַד עָשָׂר כּוֹכְבַיָּא, עֲשָׂרָה
דִבְּרַיָּא, תִּשְׁעָה יַרְחֵי לֵדָה, שְׁמוֹנָה יְמֵי
מִילָה, שִׁבְעָה יְמֵי שַׁבְּתָא, שִׁשָּׁה סִדְרֵי
מִשְׁנָה, חֲמִשָּׁה חוּמְשֵׁי תוֹרָה, אַרְבַּע
אִמָּהוֹת, שְׁלֹשָׁה אָבוֹת, שְׁנֵי לֻחוֹת
הַבְּרִית, אֶחָד אֱלֹהֵינוּ שֶׁבַּשָּׁמַיִם וּבָאָרֶץ.

שְׁנֵים עָשָׂר מִי יוֹדֵעַ? שְׁנֵים עָשָׂר אֲנִי יוֹדֵעַ: שְׁנֵים עָשָׂר שִׁבְטַיָּא, אַחַד עָשָׂר כּוֹכְבַיָּא, עֲשָׂרָה דִבְּרַיָּא, תִּשְׁעָה יַרְחֵי לֵדָה, שְׁמוֹנָה יְמֵי מִילָה, שִׁבְעָה יְמֵי שַׁבְּתָא, שִׁשָּׁה סִדְרֵי מִשְׁנָה, חֲמִשָּׁה חוּמְשֵׁי תוֹרָה, אַרְבַּע אִמָּהוֹת, שְׁלשָׁה אָבוֹת, שְׁנֵי לֻחוֹת הַבְּרִית, אֶחָד אֱלֹהֵינוּ שֶׁבַּשָּׁמַיִם וּבָאָרֶץ.

WHO KNOWS TWELVE? I know twelve: twelve are the tribes; eleven are the stars (in Joseph's dream); ten are the Ten Commandments; nine are the months of pregnancy; eight are the days of circumcision; seven are the days of the week; six are the Orders of the Mishnah; five are the books of the Torah; four are the Matriarchs; three are the Patriarchs; two are the Tablets of the Covenant; One is our God, in heaven and on earth.

שְׁלשָׁה עָשָׂר מִי יוֹדֵעַ? שְׁלשָׁה עָשָׂר אֲנִי יוֹדֵעַ: שְׁלשָׁה עָשָׂר מִדַּיָּא, שְׁנֵים עָשָׂר שִׁבְטַיָּא, אַחַד עָשָׂר כּוֹכְבַיָּא, עֲשָׂרָה דִבְּרַיָּא, תִּשְׁעָה יַרְחֵי לֵדָה, שְׁמוֹנָה יְמֵי מִילָה, שִׁבְעָה יְמֵי שַׁבְּתָא, שִׁשָּׁה סִדְרֵי מִשְׁנָה, חֲמִשָּׁה חוּמְשֵׁי תוֹרָה, אַרְבַּע אִמָּהוֹת, שְׁלשָׁה אָבוֹת, שְׁנֵי לֻחוֹת הַבְּרִית, אֶחָד אֱלֹהֵינוּ שֶׁבַּשָּׁמַיִם וּבָאָרֶץ:

WHO KNOWS THIRTEEN? I know thirteen: thirteen are the attributes of God; twelve are the tribes; eleven are the stars (in Joseph's dream); ten are the Ten Commandments; nine are the months of pregnancy; eight are the days of circumcision; seven are the days of the week; six are the Orders of the Mishnah; five are the books of the Torah; four are the Matriarchs; three are the Patriarchs; two are the Tablets of the Covenant; One is our God, in heaven and on earth.

THE DOODLED FAMILY™ in CHAD GADYA
You bought the kids WHAT for Passover!?
!
MRREOWR!!
?
?
?
?
BAA!!
GRRRR!!
YIPES!
OY!
OY!
OY!
OY!
Arf!
Arf! Arf!
MRREEOWRRR
BAAA!!

AND A HEAVENLY VOICE SAID, "NU, ENOUGH ALREADY WITH ALL THIS CHAOS!"

חַד גַּדְיָא

חַד גַּדְיָא, חַד גַּדְיָא, דִּזְבַן אַבָּא בִּתְרֵי זוּזֵי, חַד גַּדְיָא, חַד גַּדְיָא.

וַאֲתָא שׁוּנְרָא, וְאָכְלָה לְגַדְיָא, דִּזְבַן אַבָּא בִּתְרֵי זוּזֵי, חַד גַּדְיָא, חַד גַּדְיָא.

וַאֲתָא כַלְבָּא, וְנָשַׁךְ לְשׁוּנְרָא, דְּאָכְלָה לְגַדְיָא, דִּזְבַן אַבָּא בִּתְרֵי זוּזֵי, חַד גַּדְיָא, חַד גַּדְיָא.

וַאֲתָא חוּטְרָא, וְהִכָּה לְכַלְבָּא, דְּנָשַׁךְ לְשׁוּנְרָא, דְּאָכְלָה לְגַדְיָא, דִּזְבַן אַבָּא בִּתְרֵי זוּזֵי, חַד גַּדְיָא, חַד גַּדְיָא.

וַאֲתָא נוּרָא, וְשָׂרַף לְחוּטְרָא, דְּהִכָּה לְכַלְבָּא, דְּנָשַׁךְ לְשׁוּנְרָא, דְּאָכְלָה לְגַדְיָא, דִּזְבַן אַבָּא בִּתְרֵי זוּזֵי, חַד גַּדְיָא, חַד גַּדְיָא.

וַאֲתָא מַיָּא, וְכָבָה לְנוּרָא, דְּשָׂרַף לְחוּטְרָא, דְּהִכָּה לְכַלְבָּא, דְּנָשַׁךְ לְשׁוּנְרָא, דְּאָכְלָה לְגַדְיָא, דִּזְבַן אַבָּא בִּתְרֵי זוּזֵי, חַד גַּדְיָא, חַד גַּדְיָא.

A KID a kid, the father bought for two zuzim, **a kid, a kid.**

A CAT then came and devoured the kid that father bought for two zuzim, **a kid, a kid.**

A DOG then came and bit the cat, that devoured the kid that father bought for two zuzim, **a kid, a kid.**

A STICK then came, and beat the dog, that bit the cat, that devoured the kid that father bought for two zuzim, **a kid, a kid.**

A FIRE then came and burnt the stick, that beat the dog, that bit the cat, that devoured the kid that father bought for two zuzim, **a kid, a kid.**

WATER then came and quenched the fire, that burnt the stick, that beat the dog, that bit the cat, that devoured the kid that father bought for two zuzim, **a kid, a kid.**

CHAD GADYA

וַאֲתָא תוֹרָא, וְשָׁתָה לְמַיָּא, דְּכָבָה לְנוּרָא, דְּשָׂרַף
לְחוּטְרָא, דְּהִכָּה לְכַלְבָּא, דְּנָשַׁךְ לְשׁוּנְרָא, דְּאָכְלָה
לְגַדְיָא, דִּזְבַן אַבָּא בִּתְרֵי זוּזֵי, חַד גַּדְיָא, חַד גַּדְיָא.

וַאֲתָא הַשּׁוֹחֵט, וְשָׁחַט לְתוֹרָא, דְּשָׁתָה לְמַיָּא,
דְּכָבָה לְנוּרָא, דְּשָׂרַף לְחוּטְרָא, דְּהִכָּה לְכַלְבָּא,
דְּנָשַׁךְ לְשׁוּנְרָא, דְּאָכְלָה לְגַדְיָא, דִּזְבַן אַבָּא
בִּתְרֵי זוּזֵי, חַד גַּדְיָא, חַד גַּדְיָא.

וַאֲתָא מַלְאַךְ הַמָּוֶת, וְשָׁחַט לְשׁוֹחֵט, דְּשָׁחַט
לְתוֹרָא, דְּשָׁתָה לְמַיָּא, דְּכָבָה לְנוּרָא, דְּשָׂרַף
לְחוּטְרָא, דְּהִכָּה לְכַלְבָּא, דְּנָשַׁךְ לְשׁוּנְרָא,
דְּאָכְלָה לְגַדְיָא, דִּזְבַן אַבָּא בִּתְרֵי זוּזֵי,
חַד גַּדְיָא, חַד גַּדְיָא.

וַאֲתָא הַקָּדוֹשׁ בָּרוּךְ הוּא, וְשָׁחַט
לְמַלְאַךְ הַמָּוֶת, דְּשָׁחַט לְשׁוֹחֵט,
דְּשָׁחַט לְתוֹרָא, דְּשָׁתָה לְמַיָּא,
דְּכָבָה לְנוּרָא, דְּשָׂרַף לְחוּטְרָא,
דְּהִכָּה לְכַלְבָּא, דְּנָשַׁךְ לְשׁוּנְרָא,
דְּאָכְלָה לְגַדְיָא, דִּזְבַן אַבָּא
בִּתְרֵי זוּזֵי, חַד גַּדְיָא,
חַד גַּדְיָא.

AN OX then came, and drank the water, that quenched the fire, that burnt the stick, that beat the dog, that bit the cat, that devoured the kid that father bought for two zuzim, **a kid, a kid.**

A SLAUGHTERER then came, and slaughtered the ox, that drank the water, that quenched the fire, that burnt the stick, that beat the dog, that bit the cat, that devoured the kid that father bought for two zuzim, **a kid, a kid.**

THE ANGEL OF DEATH then came and killed the slaughterer, who slaughtered the ox, that drank the water, that quenched the fire, that burnt the stick, that beat the dog, that bit the cat, that devoured the kid that father bought for two zuzim, **a kid, a kid**.

THE HOLY ONE, BLESSED IS HE, then came and slew the angel of death, who killed the slaughterer, who slaughtered the ox, that drank the water, that quenched the fire, that burnt the stick, that beat the dog, that bit the cat, that devoured the kid that father bought for two zuzim, **a kid, a kid.**

GAMES FOR PASSOVER

There are many exciting games you can play during the holiday. Some, such as "Follow the Matzah Crumbs," are strictly forbidden in the Doodle household.

On the other hand, Charades is very popular. Try the following Passover clues on friends and family — or make up your own!

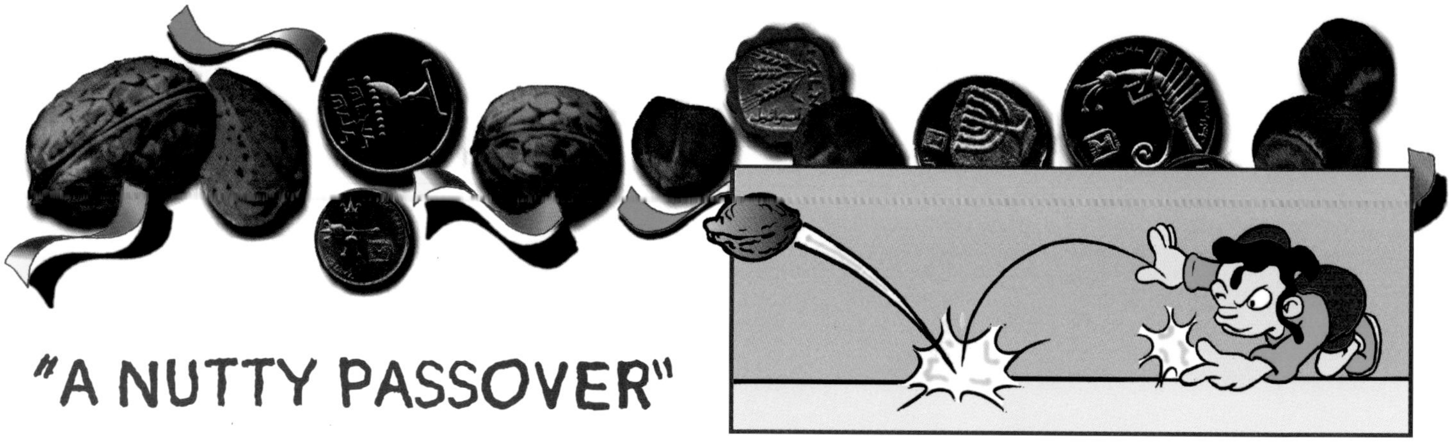

"A NUTTY PASSOVER"

Nuts are a very popular snack during Passover. They also make a great game! Stand about 10 steps in front of a wall (if inside, make sure the floor has no carpeting). Each player tries to toss a nut as close as possible to the wall. The winner takes all!

DOUBLE OR NUTTIN'

Place a bowl in the middle of the room. Players take turns throwing nuts, two at a time, into the bowl. The goal is to make one nut stay in the bowl, while making the other pop out. If both stay in or both come out, you lose the round and must leave the nuts in the bowl for the next person. If you knock one out while the other remains, you win everything in the bowl!

"TUG-O-WAR"

Spring is the perfect time to play outdoors. The game of Tug O War represents the great struggle of wills between Moses and Pharaoh. Try it with a long length of rope and two teams. And yes, it does help having Uncle Yankel on your side!

NAMES OF THE HOLIDAY

PESACH (Passover) - A reminder of how God passed over the homes of the Jews while punishing the Egyptians. "For I will go through the land of Egypt on that night, and I will destroy all the first-born... and when I see the blood, I will pass over you, and no plague will affect you when I destroy the land of Egypt." (Exodus 12:12-13)

CHAG HAMATZOT (Holiday of Matzot) - Because the Jews left Egypt in such a great hurry, they didn't have time for the bread to rise, and so they baked matzahs — unleavened bread — as commanded, "And you will observe the unleavened bread." (Exodus 12:17)

CHAG HACHEIRUT (Holiday of Freedom) - To celebrate the end of 210 years of slavery and the freedom God gave the Jews by bringing them to their own land. "Remember this day in which you went out of Egypt, out of the house of bondage." (Exodus 13:3)

CHAG HA'AVIV (Holiday of Spring) - "This day you go forth in the month of spring." (Exodus 13:4) Nissan, the month of spring and the beginning of all months, is known for other important things as well.

According to tradition, the world was created in this month; our ancestors Abraham, Isaac and Jacob were born; and the redemption will come when Elijah the prophet will blow a shofar to announce the coming of the Messiah (see page 45).

Some have the custom of saying King Solomon's Song of Songs during the Seder because it mentions the coming of spring. "...the winter is past, the rain has come and gone. The flowers appear on the earth, the time of the singing of the birds has come..." (Song of Songs: 2)

ENCYCLOPEDIA

Holy Temple

On the eve of Passover, the doors of the Holy Temple in Jerusalem were opened immediately after midnight. That custom was followed until 70 A.D., right before the destruction of the Temple. This may be why we open the door for Elijah (see page 46)

In Spain and Portugal, MARRANOS Jews were forced to convert to Christianity but secretly continued to practice Judaism. To this day, their descendants celebrate the holiday according to the ancient bible tradition. In Mexico, they smear blood on the door posts and beat streams with willows to remember Moses.

Ma'ot Chittim (Passover fund for the poor)

After his sermon on Shabbat Hagadol, Rabbi Naftali Tzvi Horowitz of Ropshitz responded to his wife's question regarding his appeal for funds: "I accomplished half of my mission. The poor agreed to accept charity from the Passover fund. All I have left to do is convince the rich to give."

Moses

Moses was one of the greatest Jews who ever lived. Though he played a crucial part in the exodus from Egypt, he is only mentioned once in the Haggadah (see page 29, "Rabbi Yose the Gallilean says..."). The lesson is, that even though we love and admire him, we must not idolize him and remember that the exodus was possible only through God's work and miracles.

Selling of Chametz

Someone once complained to the authorities that the Jews were selling chametz without paying sales tax. Emperor Franz Joseph of Austria dismissed it, saying "I know it isn't a real contract, but a religious matter." Rabbi Baruch Frankel of Leipnik sent a note of thanks, but informed him that the contract was indeed genuine and that from then on, everyone in his community would affix revenue stamps to all such contracts.

Shabbat Hagadol (The Great Sabbath)

This is the Sabbath before Passover. According to Rabbi Shneur Zalman of Liadi, author of the Tanya, we call it the Great Sabbath because we stay in synagogue longer to hear the laws of Passover and tell of its miracles. The Rome Haggadah says it was the first Shabbat the Jews began observing the commandments.

THE PASSOVER

Art

The Sarajevo Haggadah, published over 600 years ago, was the first to use illustrations. Since then art had become an important tool for showing the customs, fashions and lifestyles of the time. Some of the methods used included woodcuts, copper filigree, drawings, paintings and even cartoons!

"This must be the first Post-Modernist Haggadah"

Blood Libels

Jews were accused by anti-Semites of adding blood to their wine and matzah, since 1146 in Norwich, England, well into the 1900s in Russia and Germany.

Clothing

In Ashkenazic communities, the seder leader wears a white robe embroidered with gold and silver, known as a Kittel. Just as the seder table is our reminder of the Passover sacrifices at the alter, the Kittel reminds us of the white clothes the High Priest wore in the Temple.

- Morrocan Jews wear long white robes on the seder night to symbolize freedom.
- The rugged mountain Jews of Caucasus listen to their Elder read the Haggadah, while dressed in their best clothing and armed with their finest weapons.

Fast of the Firstborn

A day before Passover every male firstborn fasts, commemorating the miracle that the Jewish firstborn survived while the Egyptian firstborn died in the 10th plague.

ON PASSOVER EVE, RABBI LEVI ITZHAK OF BERDICHEV ASKED A NON-JEWISH STOREKEEPER: "DO YOU HAVE ANY SMUGGLED GOODS?" "AS MUCH AS YOU'D LIKE," HE ANSWERED. BUT AFTER ASKING A JEWISH MERCHANT: "DO YOU HAVE ANY BEER?", THE JEW, SHOCKED, EXCLAIMED: "THAT'S CHAMETZ!" THE RABBI LOOKED TO THE HEAVENS: "SEE HOW THEY OBSERVE YOUR COMMANDMENTS! THE MIGHTY CZAR'S SOLDIERS AND POLICE GUARD THE BORDERS, YET SMUGGLED GOODS ARE EVERYWHERE! BUT WHEN YOU SAY: 'YOU SHALL HAVE NO LEAVENED BREAD DURING PASSOVER,' YOU WON'T FIND A SCRAP OF CHAMETZ IN ANY JEWISH HOME OR STORE!

"See you in the next Doodle Family Adventure!"